Using Literature to Connect Young Adolescent Concerns Throughout the Curriculum

by
Ronnie L. Sheppard
with
Kim Ruebel
Katie Sheppard
Beverly Stratton
Diane Zigo

National Middle School Association
Westerville, Ohio

National Middle School Association
4151 Executive Parkway, Suite 300
Westerville, Ohio 43081
Telephone: (800) 528-NMSA
www.nmsa.org

Printed in the United States of America.

Sue Swaim, Executive Director
Jeff Ward, Associate Executive Director
Edward Brazee, Editor, Professional Publications
John Lounsbury, Consulting Editor, Professional Publications
April Tibbles, Director of Publications
Mary Mitchell, Designer, Editorial Assistant
Dawn Williams, Production Specialist
Mark Shumaker, Graphic Designer
Marcia Meade-Hurst, Senior Publications Representative

Library of Congress Cataloging-in-Publication Data
Sheppard, Ronnie L.
    Using literature to connect young adolescent concerns throughout the curriculum/by Ronnie L. Sheppard.
        p. cm
    Includes bibliographical references.
    ISBN 1-56090-145-4
        1. Reading (Middle school) 2. Young adult literature--Study and teaching (Middle school) 3. Middle school education--Curricula. 4. Content area reading. I. Title.

LB1632.S456 2004
428.4'071'2--dc22   2003070602

Contents

Introduction

Efforts to sustain advisory programs in many middle schools have been unsuccessful. Increased state mandates to strengthen the academic curriculum and raise test scores have taken their toll on advisory programs. Critics of these programs say that the personal concerns of young adolescents should be addressed in the home and not the school, in a time of academic accountability. Administrators and teachers continue to experience pressure to teach content, not spend time with experiences that are perceived to have little or no impact on students' academic achievement. At the same time, however, research supports the impact that middle schools, concerned with more than narrowly conceived academics, have on the lives of young adolescents. *This We Believe: Successful Schools for Young Adolescents* (National Middle School Association [NMSA], 2003) points out:

> With young adolescents, achieving academic success is
> highly dependent upon their other developmental needs also
> being met. (p. 3)

However, state and national content standards set forth bodies of knowledge that middle school students are expected to master. As a result of these external pressures, teachers and administrators face tough decisions. They struggle to find ways to increase the time devoted to content instruction, inevitably reducing time devoted to exploratory and advisory programs; or they continue the difficult task of justifying and maintaining school programs that provide guidance for young adolescents to reflect on their own developmental needs and interests.

Curriculum reforms have not been very successful in middle level schools, especially reforms that address the scope of each of the academic disciplines and what students should learn. Efforts to provide interdisciplinary and integrated curriculum in many cases have resulted in units of study that focus on fragmented facts and themes with limited connections to the disciplines. Central to effective curriculum reform is connecting what students need to learn across the curriculum, identifying real connections among these disciplines, and, more importantly, connecting the curriculum to the immediate concerns and questions of young adolescents.

> Research and practice in middle level education continue to reveal that personal and intellectual development are best achieved when treated as complementary, not separate developmental features.

The concepts found in *This We Believe: Successful Schools for Young Adolescents* (NMSA, 2003) and *From Advisory to Advocacy: Meeting Every Student's Needs* (James & Spradling, 2001) are sound. The flaw in attempts to organize and implement advisory programs is the artificial approach to this important part of middle level education. Advisory programs have too often been devoted to short and often disconnected activities that focus on topics such as self-esteem, fairness, and friendships; however, these areas have not complemented the academic curriculum. The intent of most advisory programs is to provide opportunities to meet and celebrate the unique developmental needs of young adolescents. On careful reflection, isn't it obvious that these needs should be natural parts of the school experience, not a "program" disconnected from the rest of the curriculum? Research and practice in middle level education continue to reveal that personal and intellectual development are best achieved when treated as complementary, not separate developmental features. What we teach, how we interact with young adolescents, and how we integrate the two provide very different approaches to curriculum. The basic subjects of social studies, mathematics, and language arts incorporate concepts and questions that address the concerns of young adolescents. If one examines these areas carefully, the myriad of facts and concepts leads to questions, such as, "How would our lives be different if history did not repeat itself?" "In what ways have our historical leaders demonstrated compassion, valued interactions with others, or gained trust?" "How are we affected by time and place?" and "What dilemmas were faced by Mark Twain as a young adolescent?"

I have long been convinced that literature provides a meaningful way for young adolescents to receive guidance as they reflect on their own concerns. Young adolescent novels deal with the very concerns that trouble young adolescents. Young adolescent literature brings to 10- to 15-year-olds stories that reflect the dilemmas that surface as society changes, as knowledge broadens, and as our world becomes more diverse. What has not always been obvious is that as the curriculum introduces students to more current issues and concepts, so does literature. The social sciences now expect middle school students to become more aware of geography and especially the cultures of other countries. Young adolescent literature provides stories that enrich an understanding of diversity, with, for instance, stories about life in Pakistan, youth experiencing the truths and misconceptions about judicial systems, and the continued misconceptions about learning disabilities. It also addresses those traditional concepts and skills within various academic disciplines, such as patriotism, world regions, weather and climate, economy, world population, survival, courage, trust, conflicting values, and understanding people from other cultures.

> Advisory should be an integral part of the middle school curriculum not a separate component; young adolescent literature provides a way to integrate advisory functions into the curriculum.

This publication is based on the belief that advisory should be an integral part of the middle school curriculum not a separate component; young adolescent literature provides a way to integrate advisory functions into the curriculum. Teaching and learning in the middle school can blend the concepts and skills inherent in each of the disciplines and the social, moral, intellectual, and emotional developmental needs of young adolescents. Making these connections does not ask educators to reduce time devoted to teaching the essential concepts and skills within the disciplines; rather it calls for capitalizing on the context that exists for merging the central concepts and skills for understanding one's discipline with the concerns of young adolescents. We need to identify these natural connections. A study of the United States Government readily connects to the questions young adolescents have about fairness, right and wrong, or the effects of laws on decisions we make as we grow up. For instance, in the novel, *Tangerine* (Bloor, 2001)*,* readers experience a story that connects an understanding of the judicial system to tough decisions young people have to make as they encounter crises.

The challenge for teachers is to identify young adolescent books that provide this natural connection between disciplinary concepts and skills and the concerns of young adolescents. This book identifies many such books and provides specific examples along with a model that merges advisory into and across the curriculum. ⌐

1. Academic Preparation vs. Personal Development: A False Dichotomy?

In response to *Turning Points: Preparing American Youth for the 21st Century* (Carnegie Council on Adolescent Development, 1989), schools worked to create environments that support young adolescent development. That landmark report alerted schools and communities to the need to examine the alarming societal changes and conditions that place young adolescents at risk. More recently schools have struggled with local, state, and federal mandates that address academic preparation as measured by test scores. As a result of these mandates, advisory and exploratory programs have been targets for cutbacks. School personnel, in the midst of increased pressures to meet various mandates, struggle with trying to balance a strong academic program with programs that support the personal development of youth. Unfortunately, many schools have abandoned programs devoted primarily to personal and social guidance. Nevertheless, data accumulated since the release of *Turning Points* justify the need for schools to meet all the developmental needs of American youth.

Evidence confirms the reality that most middle school classrooms still emphasize passive learning, with active and interactive instructional approaches used infrequently. Limited time is spent providing avenues for young adolescents to explore questions, participate in discovery activities, ponder important issues, apply their learning to authentic situations, and address some of their own questions about themselves, the community, and the world. However, developmental psychology affirms that during the middle school years, youth experiment, ask questions, consider alternatives, and attempt to sort out the inconsistencies they experience as they grow up. This period of transition is one when young adolescents form attitudes and beliefs, explore options, and establish a framework for making decisions as they reach adulthood. The Carnegie Corporation's follow-up report, *Turning Points 2000: Educating Adolescents in the 21st Century* (Jackson & Davis, 2000) emphasized the need to provide opportunities for young adolescents to consider new social roles, develop personal beliefs, and establish a guide for one's behavior.

It is ironic that the new national standards in the social sciences proposed by the National Council for the Social Studies (1997) emphasize a curriculum that assists youth in understanding time and place, continuity, change, conflict, people, individual identity, civic responsibility, and diverse cultures. Other national professional organizations also advocate discipline-based curriculum that is counter to school reform mandates with their emphasis on acquiring knowledge needed for success on standardized tests. These national organizations advocate conceptual approaches to the study of one's discipline, yet the type of teaching and learning that exists in many middle schools, particularly because of the pressure to perform well on paper and pencil tests, continues to be both content and teacher centered. The content standards for science (National Research Council, 1996) call for youth to know how to relate science concepts to their own lives, understand human values and needs, engage in scientific inquiry, and recognize the relationships of science concepts to community resources. Consistent is the need to provide in the content disciplines and in the total program guidance that will help youth make good decisions that are critical to their lives.

> Professional organizations in various disciplines also advocate discipline-based curriculum that is counter to school reform mandates with their emphasis on acquiring knowledge needed for success on standardized tests.

Evidence affirms the reality that youth may complete schooling successfully with its facts and figures but when faced with high-risk lifestyles that are incompatible with diverse social institutions, they may fail. The challenge is to provide opportunities for youth to understand

and apply the knowledge and skills acquired in school and to think critically and reflect on those profound questions about morality, worth, ethics, and relationships. True, high academic standards are important in providing a sound middle level education. However, the question is, What does a "high academic standard" mean? Is it rote memorization of fragmented facts and data, or is it an understanding of how to discover, how to apply knowledge in solving real problems, how to make decisions, and how to evaluate new information? Isn't it intellectual development when we ask youth to think creatively, to identify and solve problems, to communicate and work with others, and to develop skills through which they can continue to learn as the world becomes more complex?

The purported controversy between cognitive development and affective development is artificial. Middle level education seeks to emphasize, not de-emphasize, academic excellence. Long-term research on learning indicates that discussion, questioning, inquiry, conflict resolution, critical thinking, and reasoning enhance learning. These intellectual experiences have typically been viewed as central components of an academic curriculum. One problem with advisory programs has been a lack of understanding of just what is meant by advisory. Questions such as these need to be discussed and answered: How can advisory connect to the middle school curriculum? What are teacher responsibilities? How can advisory support academic achievement?

> The purported controversy between cognitive development and affective development is artificial. Middle level education seeks to emphasize, not de-emphasize, academic excellence.

Advisory, a natural part of the academic curriculum, not an isolated component

A look at the national standards proposed by each of the academic disciplines reveals that abilities such as inquiry, problem solving, and critical thinking are natural ingredients of an effective advisory program. Such skills form the basis of a strong middle school curriculum.

Too often, academic standards, as well as fragmented advisory programs, are not focused on the big ideas within or across the curriculum. Discrete facts do not address the larger concepts that connect what youth are learning to real issues. Middle school students continue to be expected to learn an impossible number of disconnected facts, demonstrate learning in isolated assignments, and master meaningless skills. To teachers and students, the sheer number of standards seems impossible to achieve. Embedded in the academic disciplines, however, are great ideas that provide natural connections to key issues that concern youth, such as diversity, self-confidence, relationships, adjusting to change, identity, trust, companionship, and human nature.

> Embedded in the academic disciplines are great ideas that provide natural connections to key issues that concern youth, such as diversity, self-confidence, relationships, adjusting to change, identity, trust, companionship, and human nature.

A curriculum that is grounded in an integration of great ideas and skills with the questions and concerns of youth is genuinely authentic. Such a curriculum speaks to both the national concern that youth are ill-prepared within each discipline and the continuing needs of young adolescents as they change intellectually, personally, socially, and physically. The great ideas found in the disciplines should frame the curriculum. They provide young learners an anchor for organizing thoughts and shaping personal meanings as they attempt to figure out the world around them. One must look at these disciplinary concepts and ask: What do students in this discipline need to know in order to face compelling challenges now and in the future? How will the study of this discipline help students become informed and cooperative citizens? How can students become self-directed and lifelong learners?

Beane (1997) believes that integrating student concerns with learning makes the curriculum more accessible and culturally relevant.

If students make the connections that exist between concepts that guide each academic discipline and their concerns, the curriculum becomes meaningful. The premise driving this book is that a school curriculum that artificially separates academic preparation and advisory experiences is doing what is both unnecessary and ineffective. If one views these disciplines as natural contexts for discovering, reasoning, critical thinking, comparing, and synthesizing, then advisory experiences become central components within the total curriculum.

> A school curriculum that artificially separates academic preparation and advisory experiences is doing what is both unnecessary and ineffective.

Consider this example: In the book *Seedfolks* (Fleischman, 1998), a young adolescent encounters personal and interpersonal problems as she struggles with moral decisions. We know that young adolescents are at a time when moral, physical, intellectual, and social growth become intertwined, each affecting the other. It is too simplistic to categorize their questions about right and wrong simply as a moral dilemma. In truth, the issue may stem from inconsistencies young adolescents experience in their social lives. At the same time, their questions concerning family relationships may be rooted in their limited experience in reasoning, problem solving, and considering multiple points of view. Growing up involves change, questioning, experimentation, fluid actions, and reactions. A book such as *Seedfolks* provides the perspective young adolescents need as they face complex issues. It helps them understand that what they are experiencing is not a new phenomenon, but one that can be traced through history, a natural part of the human experience. Literature is both an effective and a safe way for 10- to 15-year-olds to deal with the dilemmas they inevitably face.

Thirty-minute segments of the school day devoted to advisory often lead to negative impressions. Young adolescents need to see the concepts dealt with in advisory programs connected to what they are learning in history, English, mathematics, technology, health, physical education, art, and music. To separate these is to portray a world that is easily divided into isolated bits of knowledge. However, if we are to promote critical thinking and more substantial long-lasting understandings, students need to realize that the world is a blend of culture, languages, history, values, economics, places – an array of connected concepts that helps us make sense out of the world.

There are numerous questions that must be asked and answered in order to determine how to organize a middle school curriculum so that advisory and academic preparation become a natural, integrated whole. Following are several such questions:

- How does the curriculum engage students in the big ideas of a discipline, ideas that are connected to the concerns of youth?

- Does the curriculum provide students opportunities to pose questions, synthesize information, and participate in active discussions of key ideas?

- Does the curriculum engage students in reflection, decision making, and link key academic concepts and skills to real life problems and issues?

- Does the curriculum reflect great ideas that cross disciplines and provide a context for isolated facts?

- Does the curriculum provide instruction in constructing knowledge and engaging youth in higher order thinking?

- Does the curriculum use the richness of each academic discipline to expose students to differing points of view and link these to concerns youth face as they grow toward adulthood?

- Does the curriculum help youth in developing attitudes and values?

Perhaps the demise of many advisory programs is tied to the word "program." A program signifies a separate entity, an add-on; and treated that way it has often failed to gain the support of students, their parents, and even faculty. Although the objectives were valid, the means did not prove wholly satisfactory.

Using young adolescent literature to integrate advisory across the curriculum

The rich stories included in this resource provide natural links to much of what is current in the concepts that connect social studies, science, mathematics, and language arts. Youth encounter in their study of history and geography an array of events, situations, and people who have shaped the world. What is not always so obvious to young learners is that these same situations are reinvented in the events and people who surround their own lives. Only place and time divide them. What is even less obvious is that the concepts that give real meaning to the social sciences are also intertwined with the concepts that face the ever-changing world of science, with a rich history of environmental changes, scientific discoveries, adaptations to discoveries about the earth, the human body, and natural resources. Always connected to these historical, geographic, economic, and scientific changes is the power of communication – the richness of language and literature. As young people encounter changes in the world, a language is needed to internalize those changes and communicate with others. As always, literature has served as a medium through which to reflect the present, the past, and predict the future. Embedded in current biographies, fiction, drama, and essays are thoughts of others, the events that take place around us, and the concepts that provide a foundation for curricular change in our middle schools.

As young adolescent literature is introduced to young people, their parents, and teachers, concepts from the various disciplines are blended with opportunities to reflect on one's own growth. As these stories unfold, young adolescents encounter the diversity among people who struggle to answer their own questions, such as the Vietnamese girl in *Seedfolks* (Fleischman, 1998) as she begins to reflect on social issues that surface as communities change and how people find positive ways to reach out to one another or to respond to personal problems. Such a story provides a mirror of those same struggles as young adolescents examine the history of other locations, such as Asia, Egypt, and Africa or attempt to make sense out of the myriad changes in the geography of the world.

To understand key wars that affected our world, young people begin to see through the eyes of youth. For example, the story of Toby in *When Zachary Beaver Came to Town* (Holt, 2001) reveals the effects of the Vietnam War and how war often challenges youth to recognize what is important in life. Young readers begin to understand the differences between growing up in rural locations and in urban areas when they read *Dovey Coe* (Dowell, 2001). They witness the pride young adolescents feel as they begin to value who they are, even if they are different from those they encounter in school or in their travels. What a gift to be able to focus on a young person's concern about fairness and how to face a world that is not always fair as in *Holes* (Sachar, 2000), or to experience the tragedies of prejudice as depicted in *The Watsons Go to Birmingham* (Curtis, 1995) and how a critical period in history can affect ordinary, individual lives.

What is apparent as we read fiction written for young adolescents is that universal themes are found in literature – themes that provide a foundation for those "big ideas" young people encounter in school. For example, the notion of courage, how to become courageous, and the struggles of being courageous become significant as students study the Civil War, the American Revolution, and health issues such as AIDS, smallpox, and diphtheria. Young adolescent stories offer opportunities to explore facts and ideas associated with understanding the human body in science, the environmental protection issues we face with new knowledge about nuclear waste, depletion of the ozone, and other changing events as we try to understand the meaning of physical or life science.

Diversity – An organizing theme for integrating advisory across the curriculum

Understanding diversity is a central ingredient in a responsive school environment for young adolescents. The mobility of people in the United States, recent events following September 11, and data regarding the demographics of middle schools across the country provide sound bases for offering school experiences that deal with the importance of young adolescents' strengthening their understanding and respect for differences among people. Diversity stretches well beyond cultural diversity to include physical diversity, emotional diversity, diversity within relationships, diversity in experiences and interests, and diversity in time and place. An understanding of such differences helps young adolescents understand themselves, as well as the world. In most cases, their view of the world is limited to their own experiences. Yet, in today's world they will encounter even more diversity. Myths about diversity exist and lead to more confusion in young adolescents' lives as they attempt to determine the value of diversity. What they must experience are the positive aspects of diversity while recognizing the problems that occur as they encounter differences. Such views are often difficult for students to conceptualize, especially if they experience conflicting views in their own lives from people around them. Experiences gained through books encourage young adolescents to value the richness of diversity and help them realize that diversity makes us stronger and prepares us to act in caring ways.

Schools provide a context for all children to learn, with high expectations for all. The belief that young adolescents are less able or ready to learn must be eliminated. Enormous differences among young adolescents provide a richness to classrooms; however, attempts must be made to provide opportunities for young people in the process of intellectual, social, and moral transition to examine differences, reflect on their meaning and worth, and begin to form their own perspectives. This challenge is not just for advisory programs. Those same differences exist within the core academic curriculum, where young adolescents spend the majority of their days. This resource intends to integrate in natural ways the theme of diversity and provide opportunities to build connections between diversity and the myriad concepts and skills being learned in social studies, science, mathematics, and language arts.

How can we really learn geography without understanding the concept of diversity of place and time or the impact time and place have on those who live in any part of the world – past or present? How can we understand language and the art of communication (oral and written expression) without a clear understanding and appreciation for diversity?

How can we understand and grasp the big ideas in science (past and present) unless we have a sense of diversity? For example, to understand diversity is to understand those who face disease and famine in locations in the world where there is limited medical care or the ability to adapt to a changing environment and health issues. How can we understand the motivation for historical and world events without an understanding and knowledge of governmental organizations, class systems, economics, judicial system, values, and beliefs about war? Consider the recent emphasis in our country on terrorism. What is more appropriate than to address diversity as we examine the world problem of terrorism? How can we understand logic and reasoning in mathematics and the different applications of mathematics to real-world problem solving without an understanding of differences?

It is a rare book that does not portray young adolescent characters engaged in a dilemma somehow linked to diversity – family differences, differing points of view, differing values, differing experiences, or economic differences. Diversity is a broad concept associated with self-identity, cultures, interests, experiences, relationships, historical events, and other broad concepts that characterize various subject areas. Included here are stories about young people in urban and rural America, different geographic locations, war-riddled countries such as Pakistan, India, and Vietnam. Other stories bring to youth an understanding of the questions and concerns that youth faced in times past, such as during the Civil War or the Civil Rights Movement of the 1960s. Stories raise questions about understanding oneself and understanding those who face enormous challenges with physical handicaps or ethnic stereotyping. These stories provide the anchor for a series of instructional units that connect the concepts and skills within the academic curriculum to these understandings about growing up.

Merging advisory experiences across the curriculum

The young adolescent books cited and described in this publication are organized into two chapters. One features books dealing with the theme Trust and Relationships, while the other contains books related to the theme Courage and Integrity. Each of the clusters includes descriptions of young adolescent novels that provide a foundation for instructional units that merge advisory experiences, concepts, and skills within one or more subject areas and *Turning Points 2000* (Jackson & Davis, 2000) themes. Within each unit are recommended instructional activities that engage young adolescents in reading, research, critical thinking, reflection, and problem solving. The experiences are intentionally broad and generic so teachers or teams may adapt the unit ideas and learning experiences to particular situations.

This publication does not intend to restrict one's study to only these themes. Each novel could have easily been directed to one of the additional themes of diversity in constructing the units. Teachers have an opportunity to align the big ideas in their own disciplines to an aspect of diversity that helps them to merge advisory experiences. The same is true of the introductory, culminating, and enrichment activities. Additional questions and projects could be developed to link the unit more closely with the objectives and goals of the teacher or team.

2. Literature-Based Units that Integrate Advisory Across the Curriculum
Theme I: Trust and Relationships

The examples in this and the following chapter highlight literature-based units that provide opportunities for young adolescents to reflect on their own intellectual, social, moral, and physical growth. Since the publication of *Reflections on Becoming: Fifteen Literature-Based Units for the Young Adolescent* (Sheppard & Stratton, 1993) numerous young adolescent novels have been published that provide a context for advisory experiences that reflect the concepts recommended in *Turning Points 2000: Educating Adolescents for the 21st Century* (Jackson & Davis, 2000). Each unit uses a young adolescent novel that addresses themes of diversity, with particular emphasis on trust, relationships, courage, and integrity.

The units provide a way for all middle school teachers to link advisory themes with concepts and skills addressed in core disciplines. The examples represent multiple types of units, ranging from units for a single discipline, units that focus on a specific novel study, units organized around one advisory theme, and multidisciplinary or interdisciplinary units.

Because the concerns of young adolescents are inherent in human nature, teachers will find that significant ideas within any discipline have natural connections to these concerns. Advisory themes are commonly associated with issues in social studies and literature. In many cases, however, these themes are applicable to science, mathematics, or other disciplines. Since this book advocates using young adolescent novels as a vehicle for planning units, the idea of merging advisory into the curriculum is most applicable to language arts, with special adaptability to a school reading program. To integrate advisory into an existing middle school literature or reading program is, perhaps, the most obvious approach, since a central part of any strong reading program is the selection of significant literature.

The introductory or culminating journal writings, class discussions, and enrichment activities or projects described below provide each teacher or instructional team with generic activities that are linked to all the literature selections and unit activities. They provide teachers with a framework for constructing a unit rather than describing a unit that may not be applicable to a particular population or segment of the curriculum. The units are designed as guides, with the intent that teachers will link the unit components to a topic or theme within one or more disciplines. Ideas for each discipline are included in each of the units, along with a brief summary of the young adolescent novel. Each book summary is written to address the central theme (trust and relationships, or courage and integrity). The summaries give a brief description of the story, with special emphasis on the young adolescent characters and the dilemmas they face as they discover that growing up involves responding to issues related to trust, relationships, courage, and integrity.

Among the collection of 14 young adolescent novels, diversity is a central thematic strand. Characters and stories bring to the reader those issues that concern diverse young adolescents. Special attention has been given to include books with characters that represent a range of cultural backgrounds: Vietnamese, Indian, Asian, rural areas of America, as well as youth growing up during significant historical events, the Civil War, the Vietnam War, and the Great Depression.

Each unit includes sample activities that could be developed in one or more subject areas and expanded and tailored to additional subject-based topics or themes. Teachers are encouraged to use the structure of the units as a foundation or guide for developing their own units for their subject, student population, and grade level. In addition, as one plans a unit, many of the activities listed could be adapted to use across units; therefore, ideas listed in Unit 1 could be adapted for use in Units 2-14.

Chapter 4 provides teachers with a process for identifying and developing additional units, using a range of discipline-based concepts, additional young adolescent novels, and other advisory themes that reflect the intellectual, social, emotional, and moral development of young adolescents.

Each instructional unit is connected to the *Turning Points 2000* (Jackson & Davis, 2000) themes; however, because of the interdisciplinary nature of each theme, subject-area teachers or teams may provide introductory or culminating activities and enrichment projects appropriate to that unit. Following are examples of activities that could be used within each unit. Activities are divided into journal writing or class discussion questions and enrichment projects. The activities are generic and could be expanded or combined. In addition, journal writing, discussion questions, or enrichment activities could be constructed to address specific groups of students or goals of the units.

Establishing trust and lasting relationships

Young adolescents know very clearly their own need to socialize and feel accepted. Like most new experiences, socialization is a complex process. The dynamics of forming relationships are best learned in situations where individuals want to belong and understand others.

The process of forming relationships evolves as children begin to break away from parents and establish their own identities while at the same time retaining those links they need to significant adults. Disappointments appear as young people discover that relationships change and that forming relationships is in itself a process that brings with it inconsistencies and diverse sets of rules and expectations. Trust becomes a central factor. In a world that is imperfect, young adolescents struggle with the inconsistencies they see and experience. They are often placed in situations they are ill-equipped to handle. No longer can children rely on relationships among adults to be carefree and easy to describe. Social changes result in an even more complex world.

The fluidity of relationships among young people brings frustrations and disappointments. There are both positive experiences and traumatic experiences that are difficult to understand resulting from attempts by young adolescents to discover their own identities. They search for individual uniqueness yet desire to be a part of a social group.

Young people experiment with settling on their own values, beliefs, and attitudes. For many young adolescents, this search is frightening and riddled with risks. The desire to establish their own set of rules and at the same time maintain links to family often result in erratic behaviors. With this search often comes disappointment as they test various behaviors in search of a personal identity and acceptance. Too often, children do not understand why they are unable to fulfill their own needs. Their attempts to be aggressive, form opinions, select their own interests, and respond to personal conflicts often lead to failure.

They are likely to discover that relationships are not what they thought. Young adolescents form relationships and perceptions of self and others based on false information brought to them from home, friends, school, and the media. Questions surface as they come in contact with these differences. Such experiences not only help to build healthy relationships, but also clarify who they are and help them build respect for their own individual differences.

Stories that recognize the complexities of developing trust and relationships

No question that occupies the minds of young adolescents should be viewed as too difficult to examine. Through relationships with family and friends, young adolescents create a sense of belonging. While all people may not share the same personal beliefs and values, they all share basic human needs.

Young adolescent novels provide a window through which relationships and the struggles to gain trust can be viewed. In *Seedfolks,* Paul Fleischman (1998) tells the story of a community garden project in an urban neighborhood. A neighborhood comes together and grows in trust and respect as individuals realize how much they have in common. Kim, a young Vietnamese girl, comes to know her neighbors from Asia, Latin America, and the Caribbean. This story, like other young adolescent stories, is rich in its emphasis on relationships and the power of trust among people from differing backgrounds and experiences.

The Watsons Go to Birmingham (Curtis, 1995) is a touching story of how adolescents develop compassion for others as they struggle for independence. These two stories represent what is real about growing up in a world of diversity, and they provide key ideas that connect the disciplines. *When Zachary Beaver Came to Town* (Holt, 2001) gives us a view of the 70s and growing up in a small town with the backdrop of the Vietnam War. The story explains organic farming techniques and the causes and problems of obesity as well.

Even though young people do not generally like history, *Dovey Coe* (Dowell, 2001) is a thriller, a mystery, and a memoir of a time gone by. The book centers on how families are strengthened and how goals are formed and sustained. Readers will encouter forensic science, the miracles of healing herbs, and the struggle of an individual coming to grips with deafness. The adventures of the sea come to life in *The Wanderer* (Creech, 2002) along with the search for self-satisfaction and an understanding of one's heritage. Marine science, machinery, and the wonders of an adventurous girl provide a context for connecting science and social studies. The struggles of the Great Depression are seen in *A Year Down Yonder* (Peck, 2000) and *Bud, Not Buddy* (Curtis, 2002). Technology becomes real as readers gain a sense of then and now, with references to indoor plumbing, portable radios, and the cost of food.

Each of these stories provides what is often missing in the standard curriculum, real stories about real people. Through these stories trust is the key to forming strong relationships. Such a concept is shown as the key for much of what has happened in the world. Discoveries in science, mathematics, communication, and social interactions have occurred as the world became closer and individuals discovered that relationships and trust lead to new and better ideas. However, each captures realistic views, highlighting the struggles to develop the trust needed for meaningful relationships. Each story provides multiple avenues to engage young adolescents in reflecting on the complexities of establishing relationships and trust. Each story also provides opportunities to ponder additional young adolescent concerns and brings forward the realities, complexities, and universality of relationships.

UNIT 1

Seedfolks

by
Paul Fleischman

HarperCollins
Children's Books

*Solving personal
and interpersonal
problems through
positive and
constructive
solutions requires
respect and trust.*

Seedfolks tells the story of a community garden project that developed in an urban neighborhood in Cleveland, Ohio. The focus of the book is not so much on the garden but on the many residents of the neighborhood who come together, growing in trust and respect as they realize how much they have in common. Each chapter is told from the first-person perspective of a different member of the neighborhood community. Narrators represent a wide range of cultures reflecting the reality of many contemporary American neighborhoods. Some characters are recent immigrants from Asia, Latin America, or the Caribbean. Others are the now elderly descendants of an earlier generation of immigrants from Eastern Europe. Still others are African Americans who are long-time residents of the neighborhood with family ties in the South.

The tale begins as Kim, a lonely young Vietnamese girl, plants six bean seeds in a trash-filled vacant lot as a memorial to her deceased father. She is observed by Ana, an elderly Rumanian woman, who watches from an apartment window. At first, Ana is suspicious of Kim, thinking she is hiding drugs or money in the lot. She goes down to investigate and discovers with embarrassment and then delight what Kim is doing. With each chapter, we learn how Kim's tiny bean patch evolves into a city-sponsored community garden lot. We also see how the common experience of gardening, working in the soil, caring for one's own vegetables and small plot of ground pull this diverse group of people together. For Gonzalo's uncle, Tío Juan, the garden provides him with a way to recover his dignity and sense of purpose after leaving his small village in Guatemala for an unfamiliar American city. For Virgil's father, a taxi driver from Haiti, his efforts to grow baby lettuce for upscale downtown restaurants represent a way for him to earn extra money for his family.

In addition to the individual stories of triumph and rebirth through tending the garden, the individual narrators also begin to develop relationships with one another. Many of them were initially mistrustful of each other, resenting changes in "their" neighborhood or uncomfortable around the unfamiliar languages and customs of their fellow gardeners. Over time, however, they begin exchanging gardening knowledge, sharing their first vegetables, and eventually sharing in the gentle triumphs and tragedies of one another's lives, as true neighbors do. Each story also provides rich insights into the personal struggles each character faces, with some aspect of the gardening project serving as a movement toward healing or reconciliation. The invalid, reclusive Mr. Myles finds new companionship in his daily visits to the garden. Amir, an Indian store owner, is finally accepted by neighbors who initially avoided his fabric store. The book ends after one full year, representing the complete growing cycle, as yet another neighbor watches "a little Oriental girl, with a trowel and a plastic bag of lima beans" return in the spring to plant her new crop for the year to come.

Seedfolks at first may appear to be deceptively simple. Only 69 pages long, each of its 13 short chapters contains rich character development and enough details to create a believable, sympathetic portrait of a member of the garden community. Because each chapter is written in natural, first-person prose, students will enjoy stepping into the life of each character, finding how they have much in common with the adolescents and adults whose stories unfold here.

SUGGESTED UNIT ACTIVITIES

This unit is built around studies of people from different cultures. Emphasis is placed on how individuals adapt to change. The unit also provides a study of immigrants in America as well as civic responsibilities.

Journal Writing and Class Discussions:

1. Identify journal and discussion questions (from pages 45-46) in order to connect young adolescent concerns about communication, civic responsibility, change, and trust, to the book's emphasis on

how people often find it challenging to adapt to new situations and cultures that are different. This unit provides opportunities for students to make connections between changes that exist in their own lives and changes that have become a part of our history.

2. Read other accounts about immigrants adjusting to life in America.

3. Identify and discuss real-world problems and issues related to immigration, not just patterns of immigration to America, but more personalized accounts of the reasons why people come and the challenges they face. Why do people harbor prejudices toward immigrants? How can people learn to relate in positive, respectful ways? The experiences of immigrants who came to America in the earlier years of the 20th century as well as more recent immigrants from Latin America, Asia, and the Caribbean should be included. The experiences of African Americans moving from the South to northern cities should also be studied.

4. Discuss changes in any community, new residents, new construction, new industries, differing social classes. What problems can such changes cause? What tensions arise as people try to adapt to these changes? How can people work together to find meaningful solutions?

5. Discuss community problems and issues, such as solving both personal and interpersonal problems through positive, constructive solutions.

6. Discuss the role of cooperating and collaborating in solving problems and building community. How do people in students' own communities cooperate? What kinds of problems exist in students' own neighborhoods and communities, and how might these problems be addressed?

7. Teach and apply essential critical thinking skills; for example, have students analyze the skills that were necessary to make the community garden project work.

8. Students may not have background familiarity with the setting of the story or the cultures and issues presented. Because each chapter is so short, these chapters could lend themselves effectively to instruction in reading comprehension strategies.

9. Develop a variety of writing prompts based on the numerous issues that emerge within this book. Students can create their own chapters based on research into a culture or speculate on their created character's experiences such as, What could draw this character to the garden? What would this character contribute to and gain from being part of the garden community?

10. Provide opportunities for reflection; have each story take the form of a problem or solution. What sort of personal problem did characters face that the garden helped resolve? Students could reflect on positive approaches to solving their own personal or interpersonal problems.

11. Encourage independent inquiry. Students can research issues surrounding immigration to and relocation within America in the past and present. Ideally, students should try to understand these issues not just in terms of facts and statistics, but in the ways individual lives are changed.

12. Plan school projects by having students investigate and develop plans for ways to improve a local school or community life.

UNIT 2

The Watsons Go to Birmingham

by Christopher Paul Curtis

Bantam Doubleday Dell

A story of a young man entering his teens, torn between asserting his independence and awkwardly expressing love for his family.

Kenny Watson tells the story of his family's life in the 1960s. Beginning in an unusually chilly winter in Flint, Michigan, the story introduces us to the five members of the Watson family – Kenny's mother and father, somewhat rebellious older brother Byron, and delightful little sister Joetta. Each chapter traces the realistic episodes in the life of a loving African American family, whether it is Kenny's lessons in learning what it means to be a loyal friend to a newcomer in his school or his efforts to tattle on and avoid being teased by his moody, adolescent brother. As the novel progresses, the chapters become increasingly moving as we share in the family's growing frustration and concern with Byron's increasingly disobedient behavior. Kenny himself describes his own confusion over Byron's behaviors. In Chapter 6, he thinks, "Leave it to Daddy Cool to kill a bird, then give it a funeral. Leave it to Daddy Cool to torture human kids at school all day long and never have his conscience bother him, but to feel sorry for a stupid little grayish brown bird."

Finally, Kenny's parents decide that Byron should spend the summer with his grandmother in Birmingham, Alabama, as both punishment for his latest round of misbehavior and as a chance to help Byron grow up into new responsibilities and relationships with other members of his extended family.

The novel takes a more somber turn as the family journeys south during the days of the Civil Rights Movement. Because the book is told from the point of view of Kenny, still a young child, we see these events through Kenny's often puzzled eyes. A near-drowning episode where Byron rescues Kenny prepares us for the book's climactic event, the bombing of the Sixteenth Avenue Baptist Church, where four young teenage girls lose their lives. Kenny initially fears that his little sister Joetta is among the victims. Although we soon learn that Joetta is safe, Kenny must then deal with his sudden awareness of the fragility of life and the frightening reality of a world where adults commit acts of violence against innocent children.

The book follows Kenny's increasing maturity as well as Byron's. Although Kenny cannot always understand Byron's behavior, older adolescents may be able to see Byron with the compassion intended by the author. He is a young man entering his teens, torn between asserting his independence and awkwardly expressing his love for his family. Byron is especially instrumental in helping Kenny cope with the trauma and grief of the church bombing. Kenny finally realizes that ultimately, in spite of his teasing and wisecracks, Byron loves him deeply and will never let him down.

While the book focuses upon trust and compassion among family members, it also helps show how a critical period in America's history affected ordinary lives. The book concludes with an epilogue that expands upon the historical context of the church bombing and encourages young readers to consider ways that they too can become "true American heroes" who work to right the wrongs they see in their world.

SUGGESTED UNIT ACTIVITIES

This unit provides teachers with numerous opportunities to examine how time and place influence the behaviors and beliefs of people. Such concepts as coming of age, friendship, getting along with peers, nonviolence, family relationships, diversity, and trust are significant in this unit. The unit provides a rich context for young adolescents to connect their lives with the Civil Rights Movement as they try to discover their own identity.

1. Read and discuss supplementary materials about the summer of 1963 during the time of the Civil Rights Movement along with the last chapters of this novel. Journal writings and class discussions can focus on discovering one's own identity.

2. Identify and examine real-world problems and issues, such as

- The Civil Rights Movement, its causes, actions, major incidents, and results, or the senselessness and reality of violence in our world – bombings, terrorism, alternatives to violence.

- Family relationships – getting along with brothers and sisters, parents, extended family

- Coming of age – tensions between finding one's identity and remaining true to family values and responsibilities. Dealing with peer pressure.

- Getting along with peers. Friendship – what does it mean to be a true friend?

3. Identify and discuss community problems and issues – how communities reacted to change through non-violent means.

4. Teach and apply critical thinking skills, such as

- Reading comprehension, making inferences, and point of view. Because this story is told from the point of view of a rather innocent 10-year-old, we see events from his understanding and maturity. To adult readers, it is clear that Kenny, the narrator, often misunderstands what is happening around him. He is gullible and falls for practical jokes. He jumps to conclusions without having complete information. It will be important for adolescent readers to be helped in understanding that Kenny's perspective is often incomplete or inaccurate. Students may be assisted in making inferences based on facts the author reveals to us, but Kenny doesn't understand. Students can be helped to see that Kenny's interpretations of situations are not necessarily the correct ones.

- Research facts surrounding the events of 1963. It is essential that students have a background for understanding the final chapters of the book. The author does not provide a great deal of historical background in his efforts to remain true to what a 10-year-old would know, so students will need some help in understanding the actual incident.

5. Provide opportunities for reflection. Many chapters lend themselves well to determining what is "really" going on. Is Byron the juvenile delinquent that Kenny thinks he is? Are Byron's parents making wise decisions in handling his mischief and acts of rebellion? Why does Byron change so much when the family travels to Birmingham? The final chapters are especially critical as readers piece together how the bombing of the Sixteenth Avenue Baptist Church affected Kenny and how Byron helps him cope with the trauma he has experienced.

6. Provide opportunities for independent inquiry, such as

- Researching the events of 1963 related to the Civil Rights Movement and other important national and world events that happened in that year.

- Explorations of American culture in 1963 – items and incidents referred to throughout the novel (e.g., fashion, and why Byron's hair "conk" is so upsetting to his family).

- Reviewing the recent trial of the men accused of planning and carrying out the Birmingham bombing so many years after it occurred. Explore why it took so long for the accused men to be brought to trial.

UNIT 3

Dovey Coe

by
Frances O'Roarke
Dowell

Aladdin Paperbacks

*A heartwarming
story about the
strength of families
and the importance
of integrity.*

*D*ovey Coe is a spellbinding murder mystery as well as a joyous memoir of a time gone by in the mountains of North Carolina. Dovey is a tomboy with a beautiful older sister and a deaf mute brother. Her parents have instilled in them pride in who they are and love of their beautiful mountain home. They are honest to a fault and hard working.

Dovey can be hardheaded and prickly. She tries to protect her siblings from all assaults both physical and emotional. She is completely fearless, sometimes she is a bit over the top, and once she seriously strains her relationship with her proud father who believes that his children must make their own choices. In the course of the novel Dovey comes to see the strength and wisdom of her father and experiences the depth of his love for his children.

We learn at the very beginning of the novel that there has been a murder and that Dovey is not only accused of it but had reason to hate the victim. Then Dovey goes back to the beginning and tells us how she got to this place. Eventually, she is exonerated, but the murder remains officially unsolved. In the course of the story, Dovey matures and realizes that everything is not always black or white. The death of Dovey's villain and the true sorrow of his family make her realize the value of every life. Her smart, young attorney helps her see the reality of the charges against her and the possible consequences of them.

In this humorous, exciting, and heartwarming story we learn about the strength of families and the importance of integrity and courage; we also learn that goals are important and should not be easily abandoned. Readers get a realistic picture of life in rural, mountainous North Carolina before the progress of the late 20th century has begun.

SUGGESTED UNIT ACTIVITIES

This novel provides an opportunity for teams to plan an interdisciplinary or thematic unit on trust and relationships.

Language Arts

1. Journal writing, discussion questions, and enrichment projects on pages 45-48 provide opportunities for students to begin to gain a sense of what it means to trust – to form relationships among people.

2. Write the *Ballad of Dovey Coe.* Include in the ballad how the character reflected a sense of trust.

3. Pick two characters who seem diametrically opposite of each other and contrast them in an essay. Essays should focus on character traits that reflect trust and relationships.

4. Using what the story tells you, draw a picture of Coe's house.

5. Describe Caroline's going away party in the form of an article in the local newspaper. Use editorial style to reflect how relationships are important.

6. Write an essay about Dovey's strengths and weaknesses.

7. Develop a dictionary of "mountain talk."

Social Studies

1. Describe the Appalachian Mountains in North Carolina. How are relationships formed in an area that has close family ties and customs? How is "trust" significant to the livelihood of Appalachian residents?

2. How does the culture of a hill people differ from that of an urban setting during the same era as the book? What is significant about understanding cultures in order to understand one's actions and beliefs.

3. What essential evidence did the lawyer and Dovey miss at first in the trial? How was it resolved?

4. How was Dovey treated differently from an adult accused of the same crime? Is this justified? What are other situations that reflect how different people are treated differently?

5. How did the victim's family and the district attorney try to turn the judge against Dovey?

Science

1. Research healing herbs such as those found in North Carolina by Dovey and Amos.

2. How does the human ear work and what are the main causes of deafness in humans?

3. Research the tools of forensic science. How might Dovey have been cleared of the crime today?

Mathematics

1. List items that the average student in your class can lift. Estimate their weight and then find the actual weight. What is the heaviest item that anyone in your class can lift over his or her head? Involve the physical education teacher in carrying out this activity.

2. Prepare a pie graph of how you think Dovey and Amos spend their days in the summer. Use amounts as well as percentages of time to prepare your graph.

UNIT 4

The Wanderer

by Sharon Creech

HarperCollins

Sharon Creech eloquently shares the ebb and flow of a teenager's fascination with the sea and her loyalty to family.

The sea, the sea, the sea. It rolled and rolled and called to me. Come in, it said, come in (p. 1).

Sharon Creech eloquently shows the ebb and flow of a teenager's life in *The Wanderer.* The lead character, Sophie, describes the slow, meandering way of life in her town by describing a river that runs through the community. She longs for the sea, which is enormous, and tinged with white waves, and full of life. When her three uncles and two cousins decide to sail from their home in the United States, across the Atlantic Ocean to Ireland, and then to England to visit Sophie's grandfather, Bompie, Sophie pleads and protests until she wins a place on the 45-foot sailboat. She's the only girl, and Uncle Mo and Uncle Stew really do not want her to come along. But Sophie is obsessed with the idea of the ocean. Something mysterious about her past and water is alluded to early in the story, but the reader is left to wonder as the boat wanders out to sea, because even Sophie does not completely understand why making this trip is so important. She feels the ebb and flow of the sea, like the sea is calling her, but also feels that something is pulling her back at the same time. The one thing Sophie knows for certain is that sailing to Ireland in Uncle Dock's 45-foot sailboat, *The Wanderer,* to visit her grandfather is something she has to do.

The voyage begins as planned – beautiful and exciting. Sophie sleeps out on deck, under the stars. She describes her two cousins, Cody and Brian, as complete opposites. "Cody is loud, impulsive, and charming in a way my mother does not trust," and "Brian – quiet, studious, serious Brian" (p. 5). The story is told through journal entries written by Sophie and later by Cody. On board, everybody seems to have trouble getting along. Uncle Stew and Brian are bossy, they make lists of what everyone is supposed to do, and they yell at Cody for joking around. Cody's father, Uncle Mo, calls Cody a "knuckle headed doofus."

Uncle Stew decides that everyone has to teach something to the others during the trip. Cody teaches them how to juggle. Only Uncle Dock and Sophie really try to learn. Everyone else thinks it's a stupid thing to do. Sophie decides to teach her relatives the stories that Bompie has told her. And she tells great stories about Bompie. The only thing, Cody tells the reader in a journal entry, is that Sophie has never met Bompie. And her parents aren't really her parents. They adopted her. Brian needles her all the time about being an orphan, but Sophie acts like she isn't one. And she insists that Bompie told her the stories.

The mystery of Sophie's past bugs Brian. He thinks Sophie lives in a dream world and makes things up. Cody feels sorry for her and wants to know what happened to her real parents. This becomes very important the closer they get to England. Sophie is scared about seeing Bompie, but she doesn't know why. Then a terrible storm engulfs the sailboat, and they all fight for their lives. Sophie's nightmares merge with real life when a gigantic wave rises up out of the ocean and sweeps over the boat. Suspense builds and builds as the reader wonders if they will survive and just what Sophie will discover about herself on this journey.

The Wanderer is an adventure-filled story of a bold and daring girl's journey across the ocean and into the memories of her past. Sophie's struggle to reclaim who she is provokes similar struggles from those around her.

SUGGESTED UNIT ACTIVITIES

This unit is designed for language arts or reading, with suggested extensions for social studies and science.

1. Selected introductory or culminating journal writings, class discussions, or enrichment projects on pages 45-48 are appropriate for connecting students' personal encounters, beliefs, and attitudes

of trust, relationships, self-identity, and diversity, to content and literature unit activities.

2. Journal writing: Cousin Cody writes his own journal entries and reveals that Sophie is an unreliable narrator and does not always tell the truth. What happened in her past? Why does Sophie tell us things that Cody says are not true? These questions will motivate readers to keep reading to discover the answers to Sophie's secrets. The book provides a context for students keeping their own journal entries much like Sophie did in the book.

3. Discussion topics:

- What are the advantages of having both Sophie and Cody take turns narrating this story? Why do you think the author did that?

- At what point do readers learn that Sophie isn't necessarily a reliable narrator?

- Sophie describes herself this way: "I am not always such a dreamy girl, listening to the sea calling me. My father calls me three-sided Sophie: one side is dreamy and romantic, one logical and down-to-earth, and the third is hardheaded and impulsive." Do you agree with this? Find parts in this story that support your opinion.

- What are some of the things that Sophie likes about sailing? How does it make her feel?

- On page 95, Sophie says, "I wondered if it was better to know about the bad things in advance and worry about them, or whether it was better not to know, so that you could enjoy yourself." What is your opinion on this topic? Give examples of when each situation might be better.

- Each of Sophie's three uncles is on his own search. Describe each uncle and what this sailing trip might mean to him.

- How is Brian different from Sophie and Cody? What are some of his good qualities?

- On page 152, Sophie reacts strongly to seeing the mother and child dolphins. Why is that?

- How does the storm affect the trip and the crew? What do we learn when Sophie describes the wave as being black? (p. 256)

- What is the significance of the Bompie stories? How does Sophie know them?

- Who does Bompie recognize first? Why is that?

- How is Sophie able to come to terms with the truth about her past?

4. The book provides opportunities to focus on voice, metaphors, point of view, and setting. Excellent examples in the book provide a natural context for studying how point of view, setting, and voice affect a story.

5. The book provides context for class discussions that speak to conflicts of growing up as they follow Sophie on her journey.

   - Relationships resulting from adoption

   - One's search for identity

   - The significance of self-esteem

   - The difficulty in making decisions about one's love of adventure and the loyalty for sustaining family relationships

   - Courage and survival

Suggested Extensions for Science and Social Studies

1. The book provides an opportunity to examine information about marine life, weather patterns, rivers, and oceans. Science teachers can provide the scientific information needed to understand the difficulties Sophie faced as she met the challenges of the sea. Social studies teachers can assist readers in understanding how the sea challenges travelers to trust nature or how the sea has the power to form relationships with those who travel on it.

2. In order to establish a context for the story, parallel studies could be undertaken to learn about the geography, cultures, and history of Ireland and England.

UNIT 5

When Zachary Beaver Came to Town

by
Kimberley Willis Holt

Yearling

A story of Toby and his discovery of the harm and good that humans do to one another.

When Zachary Beaver Came to Town is a funny and thought-provoking story of the small town of Antler, Texas. It is told through the eyes of Toby, but Zachary is the catalyst for much of the action and soul-searching that goes on in the town. Toby faces problems of his own when his mother takes off for life in the fast lane in Nashville, but they are nothing compared to the sad life of the extremely obese Zachary. As the story progresses, Toby matures and begins to see the people of the town as individuals rather than as the boring, one-dimensional characters he believed them to be. He discovers a lot about humanity during the course of his 12th summer in the Texas panhandle.

At the beginning of the story, Toby does not understand why his father has chosen life in a small town when he could have had wealth and privilege in Dallas. By the end of the story he realizes all the gifts of time and concern his father has given him. At first he wants nothing to do with Zachary Beaver, but his innate sense of kindness and fair play lead him to help make Zachary's most important wish come true. In the end of the novel he is even able to help his former romantic rival get the girl he realizes is not for him. He is finally able to forgive his mother for what he considered abandonment and make plans to visit her in Nashville. These turnarounds are not without painful steps forward and backward, but Toby is able to face his mistakes and fears and grow.

The reader learns about small town life in the early 1970s against the backdrop of the Vietnam War. Toby's best friend Cal receives letters from his lonely brother who is "in country." We also learn about strengths and weaknesses and about the harm and good that humans do to one another. Most importantly, this novel shows young people making connections with people they might in other circumstances shun or ridicule. They learn that if you take the time to get to know someone, you can see the whole person, not just the odd quirks that stick out at first. Human connections among people of all ages and stations in life occur in sleepy Antler, Texas, where "community" means something.

SUGGESTED UNIT ACTIVITIES

This young adolescent book provides multiple opportunities for teachers and instructional teams to plan and implement an interdisciplinary unit that emphasizes how individuals are affected by time and place.

Language Arts

1. Identify journal topics, discussion questions, and enrichment activities that emphasize relationships, differences among people, self-identification, and diversity.

2. Focus on point of view by having students summarize the story from Zachary's point of view.

3. Write an essay about which character changed most during the story and support it with details.

4. Write a selection called *The Ballad of Zachary Beaver*. Pay special attention to rhyme and rhythm and try to use at least one simile, metaphor, and one example each of hyperbole and onomatopoeia.

5. Make a Venn diagram comparing Toby and Cal.

6. List as many things as you can that make this setting (both time and place) distinctive. In other words, how do you know that this novel takes place in the 1970s, and what elements explain what a small Texas panhandle town is like?

Social Studies

1. Research the Vietnam War. Be sure to tell causes of the war and how long it lasted and its results. Study life dring the war in the 1970s.

2 Research the history of the military draft in the United States.

3. Research the anti-war movement during the Vietnam War.

Science

1. Explain why Cal's dad used ladybugs and no pesticides or herbicides.

2. Research organic farming techniques.

3. Find out what the causes and treatments are for extreme obesity.

4. Make a diet and exercise plan for Zachary.

Mathematics

1. Calculate the distances from Antler to Dallas, New York, and Nashville. Averaging 50 miles an hour how long would it take to reach each city by car, bus, or truck?

2. If Zachary is the same age as Cal and Toby, how many pounds did he gain a year to reach his current weight?

3. If Zachary goes on a diet, how long will it take him to get to an average weight for his age and approximate height, if he loses no more than eight pounds a month?

Unit Extensions

This novel provides an opportunity to examine concepts regarding trust and relationships:

- How to face the challenges of being overweight and continue to make and sustain relationships in the midst of peer pressure.

- How war brings people together and forms relationships.

- How we grow to trust those who are different and find good in people.

- How to address the conflict of establishing relationships with those who are different.

UNIT 6

Bud, Not Buddy

by
Christopher Paul
Curtis

Random House
Books

A story of Bud, a survivor of the foster care system of the day, and his triumph when he finds a home with love and support.

*B*ud, Not Buddy is the often hilarious but frequently poignant story of a depression era ward of the state who goes on a hunt for his long lost family. Bud has rules – the rules of the road – according to his school of hard knocks. He also has memories that help him put together clues to find what is left of his family, but not exactly the family he expected.

As the story opens we discover that Buddy lost his mother at a young age and that all he has of her is an old photograph that she hated, some rocks she had with numbers on them, and some handbills advertising bands he thinks his father might play with. These are pretty much Buddy's only possessions, which he keeps close to him in an old case. From these few clues he begins his odyssey to find his father, when he gets revenge on the cruel son in his latest foster home and knows he must run.

Bud has wisdom beyond his years and tells a kind lady that his eyes don't cry any more. He tries to live up to the hard image that he thinks will protect him, but the kindness of strangers and finally his own family break through the shell he had created. The hilarity of Bud's rules adds comic relief to the tragedy all around him and show how children see the adult world. Despite the difficulties in his life, Bud never loses hope. When he lets his guard down he is able to find people who help him at every turn.

As we follow Bud on his journey of discovery, we also find out about the conditions prevalent during the Depression, especially for African Americans and workers. We read about Hoovervilles and the efforts of Red Caps and Pullman porters to unionize. We discover that African Americans are not welcome in some Michigan towns. Yet, we also see the joyousness and humor of music and of families that may be a little different from the usual biological kind. Bud is a survivor of the foster care system of the day, but in the end he triumphs by finding a home with love and support.

SUGGESTED UNIT ACTIVITIES

This novel provides teachers and teams with a story that is rich in history and geography. The reader gains a sense of diversity and how diversity brings numerous challenges. This unit provides multiple opportunities to discover the meaning of trust.

Language Arts

1. Journal writings, class discussions, and enrichment projects on pages 45-48 provide multiple opportunities for self-expression and critical thinking.

2. Write and perform a one-person show with you as the main character, Bud.

3. Do a character file of the people in the novel.

4. Write a description of Hooverville, hopping the train, or of the restaurant Bud visits for the first time. Use as many descriptive words as you can.

5. Write a list of your own List of Rules and Things.

6. Write an additional section of the story as if Bud had stayed with the Amos family longer.

Social Studies

1. Find photographs of Hooverville and other Depression era scenes. (There are many photographs of this kind because of the work of Dorothea Lange and others.)

2. Write a report about what a Hooverville was and about which cities had them.

3. Research the causes of the Depression and how it affected American life.

4. Research the labor movement and how it was influenced by the Depression – especially the work of A. Phillip Randolph and the Pullman Car Porters.

5. Study the lives of average African Americans during this period of segregation.

6. Find out about jazz and the greats in music such as Duke Ellington during the Depression.

Science and Mathematics

1. How might Buddy have gone about finding his real family today?

2. When were the first blood transfusions begun? What conditions are required to keep blood suitable for transfusion?

3. Use maps to calculate the distances Buddy traveled to find his father.

4. Study the cost of food in restaurants then and compare it to now. Calculate the percentage of increase.

Unit Extensions

This unit is exceptionally useful for integrating concepts related to

- Relationships and the struggles of those who do not fit into a group

- The significance of one's identity

- Self-esteem and how to develop a strong self-esteem

- How trust and relationships bring people together during hardships.

UNIT 7

A Year Down Yonder

by Richard Peck

Penguin Putnam Books

A story that clearly acknowledges that there are lessons to be learned from senior citizens and grandparents.

A Newberry Medal Winner, this novel presents a story of strong characters with a rich sense of humor. The story begins in 1937 with the Great Depression a thing of the past. However, 1937 brought about an economic recession, and Mary Alice's father had lost his job. This meant that her parents had to give up their apartment and move into a "light housekeeping" room. Since these new living accommodations were only big enough for her parents, 15-year-old Mary Alice had to live with Grandma McDowell until the family could get back on its feet.

Grandma McDowell lived in a "hick town," a town that didn't even have a picture show. Living with Grandma meant no modern conveniences – no telephone, no indoor plumbing – and sleeping in a spooky, stuffy attic. In the past, a week in the summer at Grandma's would have included Mary Alice's brother, Joey. This time Mary Alice would be by herself since Joey, two years older than Mary Alice, was planting trees out west with the Civilian Conservation Corps.

With a trunk containing every stick of clothes she owned, two or three things of Mother's that fit her, plus Bootsie – her cat – and a "ten pound" Philco portable radio, Mary Alice arrived in Grandma's town. Grandma met her at the train station when the Wabash Railroad's Bluebird train steamed into town. Grandma was a full-figured woman with her white hair worn in a bun – not what you would call a welcoming woman. She had a reputation in the town for shaking up the local populace. Why even the law was afraid of her! Grandma was a real interesting person, to say the least.

During the year at Grandma's, Mary Alice experiences midnight adventures that help explain how Grandma "stretches" her food dollars as well as where she got her "ready money." Grandma also demonstrates how to deal with difficult people in unusual and often hilarious ways. When school is out and it is time for Mary Alice to return to Chicago, she suggests that she should stay with Grandma. Grandma's response, "You go home to your folks. It'll be all right. I don't lock my doors . . ." Mary Alice learns that Grandma "had eyes in the back of her heart." The story concludes with a wedding in "the last year of the war" and they "lived happily ever after."

SUGGESTED UNIT ACTIVITIES

This unit brings to young readers a story that reflects how, even in the midst of conflict and obstacles that may seem unbearable, trust and hope establish strong relationships that last. This social studies and language arts unit provides a study of the Great Depression and its aftermath.

1. Conduct an in-depth study of the Depression and its aftermath, with specific emphasis on the economic recession, employment opportunities, and the effects on the lives of individuals and families. In this study, incorporate journal writings, class discussions, and presentations that address issues, such as

   - How do young people adapt to having to sacrifice in time of difficulty?

   - How do families strengthen their dependency on each other in times of difficulty?

   - How do young people learn from their parents or grandparents?

   - What are the difficulties in fitting into a new location, community, or home?

   - What do people take for granted in times of wealth and prosperity?

2. Conduct a study of famous or ordinary individuals who have found themselves caught up in times of difficulty and how they adapted and came to understand the meaning of community,

relationships, courage, and honesty. Examples could be the pioneers, immigrants, those in war times, or natural disasters. Students could do biographical sketches of these individuals.

3. Conduct an economic study with an emphasis on goods and services. This could involve such concepts as inflation, price wars, or supply and demand and could lead to numerous activities that involve comparing prices then and now, calculating inflation, graphing economic shifts, and effects on goods and services.

4. Compose a biography of Mary Alice, reflecting her struggle to adapt to change.

5. Compose original stories set in the time of the Great Depression. Include family members struggling to survive and still retaining their courage, integrity, and values.

6. Do a community study for a selected location before, during, and after the Depression.

7. Provide opportunities for students to discuss the following concepts and how these concepts have a place in their own lives: compromise, adapting to change, sacrificing material goods, relationships between young people and adults during a time of crisis, persistence, courage in the aftermath of a crisis, and dependency. These discussions can serve as direct links between the lives of youth now and youth during moments of crisis.

8. Keep a log for a week or so on how we adapt to changes that are unpleasant.

9. Keep a log for a week that identifies what young people learn from adults. Categorize in terms of social events, intellectual matters, economics, or values.

10. Identify and research careers prior to, during, and after the Depression. How did individuals adapt at each point. What qualities were needed in order to adjust to the changes during and after the Depression?

11. This unit could be extended to include related activities in science, such as
    - Environmental changes resulting from the Depression
    - Scientific research before, during, and after the Depression
    - Scientific knowledge related to weather, medicine, and health affected by the Depression.

12. Supplementary readings, journal writings, and compositions could be completed to parallel this unit: biographies, journal writings connected to the activities listed above, original stories set during the Depression, related literature (fiction and non-fiction), simulation of newspapers written during the Depression, speeches that capture the ideas of those living during the Depression, and other language-based activities that focus on these years.

A. Questions for journal writing or class discussions

1. Why is it important to respect and value differences among people?

2. In what ways have you tried to get to know other people?

3. Is it possible to be yourself and still be accepted by others who are different from you? How?

4. Describe the difficult actions that are needed to develop positive relationships with others. How do you deal with these actions?

5. Why do relationships with your friends change?

6. Can you be friends with adults? Why? How?

7. What do you do when you feel you have been excluded from a group of which you want to be a part?

8. What does it mean to be a "family?" In what ways have you experienced this?

9. Are there adults, other than your family, you can go to when you need help? Who? Why?

10. What are some family situations you have observed that are admirable?

11. How does your family show you that you are valued?

12. What actions could you take to strengthen friendships or family relationships?

13. Do you think there are some commonalities among all people? Identify some. What are some differences?

14. Do you feel that you need to associate with people from other cultures? Why, or why not?

15. What is it about people who are different from you that you respect?

16. What makes "trust" difficult for you?

17. What are some problems that could result if you did not have friends?

18. What is the most difficult part of growing up around young people your age?

19. What is one important lesson you have learned from a friend or a family member?

20. What is the most significant obstacle in establishing friendships? Keeping friends?

B. Enrichment activities and projects

1. Compose a biographical sketch of an individual with whom you have developed a positive friendship.

2. If you could choose an ideal person to meet, who would it be? Compose a character sketch of this person.

3. Sometimes misunderstandings among friends or family occur. Describe one of these misunderstandings, and then recommend how you could regain that relationship.

4. List events you encountered over the past week that illustrates a friendship you have with someone.

5. Collect photos or construct a collage of special features of a friend.

6. Create a set of school rules that would welcome new students to your school.

7. Write a TV script about two friends and their encounters.

8. Compose questions you would ask people in order to get to know them better.

9. Write a biographical sketch of a family member or other adult whom you admire.

10. Interview classmates or people in the community to determine the three most significant qualities of a friend. Construct a graph or chart to report the top choices.

11. Pretend you travel to another country. What would be some ways to orient yourself to that culture? Compose an advertisement or article that highlights the interesting points.

12. Construct a list of dos and don'ts that represent what to do and not do to gain friends.

13. Compose an original tale that reflects an act of distrust. Then compose one that shows trust.

14. What are five important steps in building trust among your peers? What are five steps in destroying trust?

15. Create a story scene that illustrates trust between a person your age and a parent.

16. In a class of 20 people, five are from another culture. List several classroom events that would help them feel welcome and part of the group.

17. How could you help someone in your class excel in school? Describe three different approaches.

18. Locate articles in a newspaper or magazine that represent trust. Share them in some manner with the class.

19. Keep a log for one week that records your acts of friendship.

20. Compose a script or play that reflects two people your age engaged in a disagreement. Write two story endings – one that reflects positive friendships and one that reflects problems in being a friend.

21. Keep a record for one week that reflects what you did to establish or sustain trust.

C. **Additional young adolescent literature for the "Trust and Relationships" theme**

- *What Do You Do When Your Mouth Won't Open?* by Susan Pfeiffer
- *Take Wing,* by Jean Little
- *The Pistachio Prescription,* by Paula Danzinger
- *Where the Lilies Bloom,* by Vera and Bill Cleaver
- *Are You There God? It's Me, Margaret,* by Judy Blume
- *Hatchet,* by Gary Paulsen
- *Nothing's Fair in Fifth Grade,* by Barthe DeClements
- *The Cabin Faced West,* by Jean Fritz
- *Where the Red Fern Grows,* by Wilson Rawls
- *Home Before Dark,* by Sue Ellen Bridgers
- *Ramona and Her Father,* by Beverly Cleary
- *Sarah, Plain and Tall,* by Patricia MacLachlan
- *Bridge to Terabithia,* by Katherine Paterson
- *The War With Grandpa,* by Robert Kimmel Smith
- *Zeely,* by Virginia Hamilton
- *Dragonwings,* by Lawrence Yep
- *Dear Mr. Henshaw,* by Beverly Cleary
- *Dicey's Song,* by Cynthia Voight

3. Literature-Based Units that Integrate Advisory Across the Curriculum Theme II: Courage and Integrity

Change is difficult. A positive sense of self, therefore, is needed to provide a foundation for approaching new tasks, adjusting to changes, or dealing with new decisions. Yet, during the early adolescent years, feelings of inadequacy increase. Social encounters, academic expectations, adjustments to changes in the family, and altered physical characteristics bring a unique set of feelings and emotions. Adolescents often expect the worst. Their encounters with handling new experiences are often minimal; thus they fear failure. Their self-confidence, in large measure, determines how successful they will be in handling change. Shaping a strong self-image and the confidence to face new challenges, therefore, becomes central. Young adolescents need to discover that they have the skills to be successful and become contributing individuals. Adults should provide experiences that engage young adolescents in "safe" risk taking. Knowing that new experiences can be rewarding and safe allows young people to accept new responsibilities and gain a sense of self-control.

Growing up brings added responsibilities, especially as young adolescents begin to develop their own views and beliefs. Experiences become tangled as they encounter multiple viewpoints that challenge their decisions. Their vulnerability leads to confusion, questions, and disappointments, especially about ethical issues. Situations that were once taken for granted become moral issues, yet limited experience may prevent them from making decisions and facing consequences. Often, problems arise when they are not equipped to face them. Too, they see inconsistencies in how others react and actions that contradict what they were taught. They often rely on what peers say is acceptable, but this may cause frustration when they do not see these decisions as helpful. As a result, they often flounder.

Young adolescents in search of courage and integrity often become confused, find it difficult to sort out what to do, and act on impulse. They avoid making decisions in hopes that their difficulties will disappear. The years between 10-15 are ones when new thought processes evolve. The time is ripe for middle school students to become engaged in moral issues and look at these issues from varied points of view. The need to make connections among their varied experiences and to understand the interdisciplinary nature of the world are felt, yet in school little attention has been paid to helping youth meet these needs. If we want young adolescents to develop lifelong skills and become problem solvers, we must provide opportunities for them to examine authentic issues.

Interactions with young adolescents soon reveal the profound questions that occupy the minds of most young people. These questions, however, are often difficult to answer in a way that makes sense. Many of the questions deal with personal concerns that are confusing or abstract and do not have simple, concrete answers. Youth need assistance in coping with the inevitable day-to-day questions they face outside of school. Too often, however, they fear asking those questions lest they appear weak or reveal thoughts viewed by others as inappropriate.

Stories that recognize the diversity of courage and integrity

Stories for young adolescents capture the challenges they face as they explore the meaning of courage, struggle to be themselves, and sustain their integrity. For example, helping students explore Uncle Jed's choice not to fight during the Civil War in *Shades of Gray* (Reeder, 1999) provides a base for examining the realities of war, coping with change, and the benefits of nonviolence. Engaging young adolescents in the search for social and civic responsibility is central to understanding the social sciences as well as the challenges that scientists face in their search for solutions to medical, environmental, and health issues.

Understanding and appreciating the traditions and beliefs of varied cultures provides a context for history, geography, and economics.

Shabanu: Daughter of the Wind (Staples, 1991) brings a realistic view of the political tensions in Pakistan, India, and Afghanistan. The story captures one struggle, in the midst of chaos, to accept responsibility and maintain courage and integrity even though cultural differences and traditions are often misunderstood.

Holes (Sachar, 2000), a story that speaks to the human spirit, offers an opportunity to address racism, power, and loyalty and helps young people gain a stronger sense of our past, present, and future. Such a story shows how courage and integrity provide guidance in making decisions and evaluating one's values.

With the introduction of Steve Harmon in *Monster* (Myers, 2001), social studies comes alive in this story that focuses on the criminal justice system, issues related to gun control, safety, and the African American experience. As Max evolves in *Max the Mighty* (Philbrick, 1993) and *Freak the Mighty* (1998), young people begin to think about what courage means. Each story relates to the meaning of courage and integrity, how courage and integrity gain their strength, and how courage and integrity form the basis for understanding the concepts addressed as youth become engaged in studying people and places.

Each unit examines the struggles young adolescents face as they form their own values and beliefs. The characters in each of these stories. while diverse, emphasize the universality of courage and integrity and clarify how courage and integrity are grounded in the events and people one encounters. Stories in these books provide opportunities to examine the concepts addressed in understanding the various subjects. The courage embodied in each historical figure – from both western and non-western cultures – the history of scientific discoveries that have helped us understand animal and plant species, and the application of mathematical principles to the sciences and social sciences confirm the connectedness between facts and big ideas. Communication through print and non-print mediums provides us with a means through which we can explore ideas, examine beliefs, organize thoughts, and construct meaning. This natural connection between the disciplines and young adolescents' self-exploration provides a foundation for curricular experiences that help them form ideas about their development and establish bonds.

UNIT 8

Shades of Gray

by Carolyn Reeder

Aladdin Paperbacks

This novel addresses the complexities of courage and the respect that comes when one stands up for his or her beliefs.

Shades of Gray begins shortly after the end of the Civil War. The war has directly and indirectly claimed the lives of all the members of 12-year-old Will Page's immediate family. The novel begins as his family doctor takes him from the city of Winchester, Virginia, to live with the family of his mother's sister in the farmlands of the Virginia Piedmont. Will is still filled with grief over the recent loss of his family. In addition, he can barely control his bitter anger that his Aunt Ella's husband, Jed Jones, refused to fight during the Civil War. To Will, his uncle is the worst kind of traitor, a coward who saved his own life while others bravely gave theirs in defense of the Confederacy.

Will bides his time, learning to carry out the demanding chores and responsibilities of life on a poor farm, while secretly planning for his eventual return to life in Winchester. In the meantime, he grows increasingly fond of his cousin Meg and Aunt Ella and begrudgingly sees that his uncle is a hardworking man of integrity, although still a traitor in Will's eyes.

Through a series of incidents that culminates in his uncle's act of selfless charity to an injured Yankee soldier working his way back to his home in Pennsylvania, Will finally comes to understand that his uncle is anything but a coward. As Will comes to respect his uncle's courage in standing up for his beliefs, Will also learns through his encounters with a local bully that resolving conflicts without fighting can take even more courage than resorting to an endless cycle of violence and revenge. Eventually, Will must decide whether or not to take advantage of an opportunity to return to Winchester or remain with his new family on their farm.

This book deals with issues of courage on both a broad and an immediate scale. It helps readers consider the courage of soldiers who died in battle, the courage of those who struggled to save their families and farms, and of those trying to rebuild their lives after the fighting had finally ended. It also explores issues of forgiveness and compassion as the survivors recognize that amidst the destruction of the war, many individuals from either side carried out acts of kindness and restraint.

SUGGESTED UNIT ACTIVITIES

This unit emphasizes that courage and the struggle to be courageous are not only a part of growing up, but also a vital part of many individuals – young and old – who have faced the challenges that life brings. This unit focuses on a study of courage during the Civil War and brings to young readers new understandings of what it means to be courageous.

Appropriate journal writings and class discussions focus on

1. Courage, compassion, and how people struggle to sustain their own values and beliefs. (See pages 79-80.)

2. Topics for class discussion, problem solving, or small group discussions, such as
   - The reality of war – its effects on individual, ordinary lives.
   - Coping with drastic change – Will Page loses his entire family and must move to live with relatives he doesn't know and initially doesn't like.
   - Conflict resolution, especially through non-violent approaches. Facing up to bullies or gangs.
   - Maintaining one's integrity in spite of widely held popular opinions that differ from your own.
   - Coping with grief.

3. Recommended study of one's civic responsibility.
   - Relationship between the individual and the greater community, social and civic responsibility, and charity. Is Will's Uncle Jed a coward and traitor, or is he a courageous patriot? Was Will's older brother Charlie courageous? To what degree are we

responsible to family, community, and nation? To fellow human beings, whether we agree with their politics, religion, or values?

4. Ideas for developing and applying critical thinking skills.

- This book challenges readers to consider the complexities of the Civil War – the differing beliefs of the participants, the ambiguities, the many different ways that the war affected all American lives – officers, soldiers, conscripted farmers, the wealthy, the poor, slaves, women, children, the North, the South. Teachers should spend time on the historical background of the novel so students have an adequate understanding of the conflicts in the book and in history itself.

5. Recommendations for reflections – journal, class discussions, or small group work.

- Help students explore Uncle Jed's choice not to fight during the Civil War and encourage students to explore the nature of courage and responsibility from a variety of angles and in many situations relevant to their own lives.

- Trace the development of Will's character and growing maturity. Will must learn to cope with anger, grief, and selfishness.

- Consider Will's options throughout the book – should he stay with this family or try to return to his life in Winchester? How should he respond to Hank, the local bully? Does he make good decisions at the various choice points throughout the book? What factors influence his decisions?

6. Ideas for independent inquiry:

- The Civil War offers multiple topics for further study or exploration – various leaders, particular battles.

- Students could be encouraged to read and compare at least one of the many young adolescent novels or non-fiction books about the Civil War.

UNIT 9

*Shabanu:
Daughter
of the Wind*

by
Suzanne Fisher
Staples

Alfred A. Knopf

*A story that
spotlights how
growing up in a
culture with very
specific values,
traditions, and
expectations can
be difficult for
young adolescents
in the process of
discovering their
own beliefs.*

Shabanu brings adolescent readers to an unfamiliar world through the life of a family who lives in the Cholistan Desert of Pakistan. The story is told by Shabanu, the 12-year-old daughter of a family who raises and sells camels. Shabanu loves her life; she delights in the feisty personalities of the camels and enjoys the freedom and wild beauty of the desert. Unfortunately, as she approaches a marriageable age, this freedom will soon come to an end, and Shabanu will have to assume the responsibilities and proper behavior of an obedient wife and mother. We see signs of Shabanu's intelligence and strong spirit throughout the novel as well as her parents' increasing concern and anger over what seems to them to be insolence and stubbornness.

Shabanu's world changes dramatically over the course of the novel. Preparations for her older sister Phulan's wedding go terribly wrong, and a dispute with a ruthless landowner results in the death of Phulan's future husband, Hamir. The resulting negotiations and compromises reached by members of the feuding families include a decision that has serious consequences for Shabanu's own immediate future. She is torn between her duty to her family and her own passionate integrity.

This book introduces students to the traditions, joys, and challenges of life in a desert culture of Central Asia. While some aspects of this life may seem difficult and even puzzling to young American readers, the author also takes care to portray the deep love and fierce loyalties existing among extended family members. Further, the author helps readers understand that actions that may initially seem overly strict and unreasonable reflect the self-discipline and cooperation that have become essential for survival in a harsh and sometimes dangerous geographic region. In light of recent events involving the September 11th tragedy and the war in Iraq, this book may also be extremely effective in helping American youngsters understand and respect the humanity and culture of ordinary families who live their lives on the very fringes of the wars being fought in this part of the world.

Shabanu offers numerous possibilities for discussion and exploration: Muslim culture in Pakistan, family relationships during times of hardship, and what it means to be true to one's inner spirit. Students who enjoy this book and wonder what will happen to Shabanu can read the sequel, *Haveli,* which traces Shabanu's life as she enters into a marriage with an honorable man she does not love and becomes a young mother herself.

SUGGESTED UNIT ACTIVITIES

1. Real-world problems and issues for discussion:

   • Growing up in a culture with very specific values, traditions, and expectations; tensions between an individual and the greater social culture – relating with your parents when they "know what's best for you" and you have other ideas.

   • Coping with tragedy, change, loss.

   • The reality of social and political tensions in Pakistan, India, and Afghanistan; how these affect people who live in those countries and how important it is for Americans to grow in understanding of these countries and cultures.

   • An individual's responsibility to self and to society.

   • How culture and geography are interrelated – what it takes to survive as a people in a demanding environment.

   • Understanding and appreciating the traditions and beliefs of one's own family culture; students can compare the traditions of Shabanu's culture with their own.

2. Essential skills possibilities:

- Reading comprehension: Because the setting and culture of this novel will be unfamiliar to many American students, teachers can help them develop numerous reading strategies for understanding the actions, vocabulary, and images presented in the book.

- Geography skills: Use the map provided as well as other maps and geographical tools to explore the setting of the book, the climate, and its influence on the characters' lives.

- History: What is the time frame of this book? What has happened in this part of the world since the events of the story, and how might they affect the lives of a family such as Shabanu's? Consider continued drought, political unrest, refugees, threat of war between Pakistan and India.

- Cultural studies: It is very important that teachers help students read this book with sensitivity toward the Muslim culture being described and not read it with a negative bias. This book can provide students with the opportunity to learn more about the Muslim faith and how it forms the moral and ethical framework of Shabanu's family's life.

3. Suggestions for reflection using journals, discussions, and small group work:

- Shabanu's family makes numerous decisions throughout the story, but because of the culture, she is not allowed to have any say in these decisions. Students should be encouraged to reflect upon why various choices have been made (e.g., selling the family's beloved prize camel to an Afghan warrior to secure a good dowry for both daughters). Are these the best choices in the long run?

- Gender roles: How do the various women in the text live out their beliefs and values? Sharma is a particularly interesting figure – an independent woman who is respected by Shabanu's father in a culture where women are typically subservient to men. In what ways are women treated with love and respect in this culture?

- When do gender roles cause tension and difficulty? It will be important to treat this topic with sensitivity, especially if some students come from cultures where there are distinctly different expectations for men and women.

- Shabanu's future: Although there is a sequel to this book, *Haveli,* (Staples, 2003), students can speculate on what Shabanu means at the end when she states, "Rahim-sahib will reach out to me for the rest of his life and never unlock the secrets of my heart."

4. Independent inquiry activities:

- Further explorations of cultures of Central Asia, the Middle East, or other regions of the world.

- Explorations of students' own cultures. Children often see their own way of life as normal and do not always understand that their traditions have distinctive roots and histories and may look puzzling to people from other cultures. Students may use this as an opportunity to educate one another about their cultural backgrounds, celebrating the beauty and uniqueness of each one.

- Students may be encouraged to read another young adolescent book that explores a culture different from their own and then compare the books and make additional inquiries into various cultures. Students from Muslim backgrounds may wish to explain to what extent *Shabanu* accurately reflects their own cultural experiences.

UNIT 10

Holes

by Louis Sachar

Yearling

A book that is whimsical and funny at times, yet rich in the human spirit.

*H*oles is a novel that intertwines three stories that at first seem unrelated, but later prove to be integrally related. Stanley Yelnats is under a curse, or so he thinks. He finds himself at Camp Green Lake against his will, forced to dig hole after hole along with other teenagers who seem to deserve the punishment that he does not believe he deserves. Tennis shoes and the family curse were his undoing.

It is during this boring, difficult time that he becomes a physically strong person and develops into a young man who bonds with the underdog of the camp, Zero. It is through this strength of character and caring that he ends the curse his family is under. As we learn of Stanley's plight, we also learn how the family curse came to be, how Camp Green Lake became a virtual desert, and why the warden makes bad boys dig holes.

Evil in this story is personified by the macabre warden who has snake venom in her nail polish. When we find out who her parents are, we learn she is just continuing the family tradition of evildoing. However, the courage of Stanley and Zero in the face of this evil and the untiring efforts of Stanley's family to gain his release thwart the warden's plans.

This novel is about the strength of the human spirit and body, loyalty to family and friends, commitment, self-esteem, and responsibility. It touches on racism and the power of the peer group. At times it is dark and stark, but in the end the truth comes out because of the strength of Stanley and those who care about him. The book is whimsical and at times funny. It is also extremely suspenseful as the mysteries unfold. This is a book that can be enjoyed when read alone or aloud to others.

SUGGESTED UNIT ACTIVITIES:

This unit is organized as an integrated language arts, social studies, science, and math unit. Central are those concepts that connect young adolescent growth to an understanding of relationships, right and wrong, morality, and self-discovery. This novel can provide additional options for more focused units organized around one or more of the following themes: Judicial System in America, Laws that Affect Teenagers, and Prejudice.

I. Interdisciplinary comprehension questions for discussion or as journal writings:

1. What offense puts Stanley in jail? Research the law that supports this event. Is it a good law? Why?

2. How do the boys treat Stanley when he gets to Camp Green Lake? Why?

3. Why is the area called Camp Green Lake when it is dry? Explain in scientific terms. Connect to a map study to locate similar places in the world.

4. What are some of the dangers to people at the camp?

5. Why do the counselors not care if people escape?

6. Why does Zero begin to dig for Stanley? What does this say about relationships?

II. Writing ideas:

7. Describe Mr. Sir and the warden. Compose character sketches. Include the features that make a strong character sketch.

8. In a paragraph, describe what happens to Zero when he escapes and Stanley follows.

9. How does Stanley's father finally make his fortune? Is this realistic today?

10. Make a chart of each of the three stories: Stanley's, the curse, and the story of Kissin' Kate. List the characters and a brief summary; then explain how each story relates to the others.

III. Integrated social studies, research, writing, and discussion ideas:

11. Research the juvenile justice system in your state. Compare or contrast to the story.

12. Describe the prejudice experienced by Kate and her lover and compare it to the prejudice at Camp Green Lake.

13. Describe the habitat at the camp and on God's Thumb. Illustrate a habitat.

14. What is immigration? Why did Stanley's ancestors want to immigrate to America?

15. Discover how inventors get patents.

IV. Specialized math extensions:

16. Calculate the area of each hole the boys made.

17. Calculate the number of holes the boys made each year.

18. Estimate the distance from the camp to God's Thumb and tell what measures you used.

V. Specialized science extensions:

19. Find and halve a recipe for peach preserves.

20. Determine what animals you would find in a desert climate in central Texas.

21. Find out if there are any natural remedies that protect people or animals from venomous bites.

22. How does the brain process symbols when people learn to read?

23. Describe the process of fermentation.

24. Find information on poisonous lizards and snakes in the western United States.

25. What real conditions may cause desertification of an area?

Unit 11

Monster

by Walter Dean Myers

HarperCollins Children's Books

A story that brings to readers thoughts about justice, courage, survival, family, racism, and peer pressure.

Steve Harmon, 16 years old, begins the story with his jail experience in a Manhattan detention center where he is on trial for felony murder. "The best time to cry is at night, when the lights are out and someone is being beaten up and screaming for help…If anybody knows that you are crying, they'll start talking about it and soon it'll be your turn to get beat up when the lights go out." The murder charge resulted from Steve's alleged involvement with a convenience store holdup where the owner was shot and killed. The others involved claim Steve was the lookout for the convenience store robbery. Is this true, or was he merely in the wrong place at the wrong time? This thin, brown-skinned adolescent increasingly feels like an outside observer of his own life while the judge, lawyers, other inmates, and possibly his parents view him like all the rest – guilty. Steve is overwhelmed by fear – fear of the reality he faces each day in court, fear each night and day at the center, fear of the future, even fear of the past, but mostly, fear of the truth.

One word torments Steve; it plays again and again in his mind. The prosecutor called him Monster. Keeping a notebook during the trial, Steve writes a screenplay of his experience entitled *Monster*. "Sometimes I feel like I have walked into the middle of a movie. It is a strange movie with no plot and no beginning. The movie is in black and white, and grainy. Sometimes the camera moves in so close that you can't tell what is going on and you just listen to the sounds and guess…This is not a movie about bars and locked doors. It is about being alone when you are not really alone and about being scared all the time… Maybe I could make my own movie. I could write it out and play it in my head. The film will be the story of my life. No, not my life, but of this experience. I'll call it what the lady who is the prosecutor called me."

The screenplay describes the trial from Steve's point of view; he sets up each scene and includes thoughts and feelings each night about the trial and other characters. The reader is left to make decisions about Steve's guilt or innocence. A verdict is revealed, but even Steve is left to struggle with the truth. Presenting the harsh reality of making bad choices of friends and acquaintances, the author, Walter Dean Myers, provokes the reader to ask questions about issues such as justice, reality, and consequences for actions. The story is intensely suspenseful while Myers authentically portrays a teen through realistic dialect and leaves the readers in the jury box judging for themselves whether or not Steve is innocent or guilty.

SUGGESTED UNIT ACTIVITIES:

This unit, organized around the themes of trust, justice, and relationships, is devoted to understanding the judicial system and provides a strong parallel to a study of law, court systems, and those laws that affect teenagers.

1. Introduce the unit with information about the juvenile criminal justice system in America, including the courts, juvenile detention centers, and the laws.

2. Compose three questions to research about the juvenile criminal justice system in relation to youth.

3. Individual students or groups of students select one of the following for independent research and inquiry: public defenders, prosecutors, related court cases, or juvenile detention centers.

4. Have students serve as jurors (perhaps divide into various juries). Each group keeps a chart as participants as they read the book to determine what they believe or do not believe. Have a class discussion based on the results of the various juries.

While reading *Monster*, record events in the appropriate column.

Fact	Non-Fact	Rationale

5. Using the story *Monster* and information gained through some preliminary reading about the judicial system, have small groups discuss and share the following:

   • A person is guilty by association.

   • You cannot be charged with a crime if you were not directly involved in the crime itself.

   • We should be held responsible for the decisions we make.

6. Role play lawyers in the case and present arguments for both sides. Students in small groups develop a script. Discuss how the arguments are based on facts gained from research on law. How was this different from the events in the novel?

7. Questions for group discussions:

   • Is justice served in Steve's case?

   • Do you think Steve served as lookout man for the robbery? If he did, do you think he should have been charged with, or convicted of, felony murder?

   • Steve imagines the defense attorney is looking at him wondering who is the real Steve Harmon. How would you answer this question? Steve himself says he films his life to try to "look for one true image." Why do you think the question of who he is remains so important to Steve?

   • Reread the prisoners' debate about truth. Who is right? What happens to truth in the legal system? Are the lawyers seeking the truth? Which witnesses in the trial do you think were telling the truth and which were not? Review the testimony to determine what led you to form your opinions.

- What do you think of the screenplay format as a way to tell this story? When is the form most effective? When is it least effective?

8. Discuss the meanings of each of the following quotes from *Monster*:

   > *This is not a movie about bars and locked doors. It is about being alone when you are not really alone and about being scared all the time.* (pp. 3-4)

   > *It's funny, but when I'm sitting in the courtroom, I don't feel like I'm involved in the case. It's like the lawyers and the judge and everybody are doing a job that involves me, but I don't have a role. It's only when I go back to the cells that I know I'm involved.* (p. 59)

   > *All they can do is put me in jail. They can't touch my soul.* (p. 89)

   > *Half of those jurors, no matter what they said when we questioned them when we picked the jury, believed you were guilty the moment they laid eyes on you. You're young, you're Black, and you're on trial. What else do they need to know?* (pp.78-79)

   > *Seeing my dad cry like that was just so terrible. What was going on between us, me being his son and him being my dad, is pushed down and something else is moving up in its place. It's like a man looking down to see his son and seeing a monster instead.* (pp. 115-116)

   > *They are all equally guilty. The one who grabbed the cigarettes, the one who wrestled for the gun the one who checked the place to see if the coast was clear.* (p. 261)

9. Divide the class into small groups; using the book, have each group complete the following chart. Then discuss the collective responses.

What the author tells us about	What we believe about
Jail	
Trials	
Lawyers	
Family	
Justice	
Friends	
Group Reaction:	

10. After reading and studying the novel, conduct research on the judicial system, its laws, and related topics. Then engage students in discussions of the following:

- What is justice? How do I know when there is justice or fairness?

- Have you ever formed opinions about someone and later found out that your opinions were wrong and that you misjudged them? Explain. What are some assumptions you feel are made about young people your age just because you are teenagers? Why does this happen? What can you do to help prevent this?

- How can trust lead to unexpected events that are not pleasant? How can trust lead to events that are pleasant? How can you judge when to trust someone?

- How do strong, honest relationships with others help build trust and prevent misconceptions?

UNIT 12

Freak the Mighty
Scholastic Systems

---

and

Max the Mighty
Point Signature

by Rodman
Philbrick

Two novels that help us understand the meaning of courage as one struggles with imperfection, friendship, and being honest.

*F*reak the Mighty is a wonderful story of triumph over imperfection. Maxwell Kane, AKA Mad Max, Max Factor, Maxi Pad, describes himself as "learning disabled" with a "big dumb body." He meets Kevin, AKA Freak, a "crippled-up yellow-haired midget kid with a normal-sized head, but the rest of him shorter than a yardstick..." Freak has shiny braces strapped to his crooked legs and needs crutches to get around. Because Freak "doesn't weigh much" Max becomes his legs as Freak "walks high above the world" as he piggybacks on Max's shoulders. Together this unlikely pair combines Freak's "genius brain" and Max's "big dumb body" to become Freak the Mighty. Together they experience harrowing, fascinating adventures slaying dragons and fools and being involved in dangerous quests. When Kevin (Freak) experiences a medical emergency and lands in the intensive care unit of the hospital he presents Max with a blank book and instructions to "fill it up with our adventures." To dispel his depression after Kevin's death, Max writes the "unvanquished [*sic*] truth" of his and Kevin's adventures. The story concludes with Max saying, "Who knows, I might even read a few pages. No big deal."

Max the Mighty is the sequel to Rodman Philbrick's book, *Freak the Mighty*. The story is told by Maxwell Kane, the main character, who describes himself as "a big dude with a face like a moon and ears that stick out like radar scoops with humongous feet like the abdominal [*sic*] snowman." Even though he is a giant-of-a-boy, he describes himself, as "a real weenie, a yellow-bellied sapsucker, a giant wuss, a coward," who would "do just about anything to avoid a fight." His fear of fighting is related to his size. He is concerned that if he "hit somebody, they might stay hurt forever, or worse." Then "they'd haul me off to jail" just like my jailbird father.

Although he tries to avoid trouble Max finds himself coming to the aid of a "skinny red-haired girl who's maybe eleven or twelve years old" who is "screaming bloody murder" because she is being harassed by a "gang banger." The incident introduces Max to "Worm," the day "when trouble really started."

"Worm" is Rachael, the nickname of Max's new friend. She is a bookworm; she never stops reading. Sometimes she even wears a miner's hat to illuminate the printed page. It seems that she uses reading as an escape from the reality of an abusive stepfather called "the Undertaker because he dresses in black and drives this ratty old hearse."

When Max witnesses the Undertaker assaulting Rachael's mom, Max "kidnaps" Rachael and becomes a desperate criminal who is wanted by the law. They decide to journey to Chivalry, Montana, to find Worm's real dad because he will "know what to do." They travel across America meeting Dippy Hippie, an ex-school teacher who drives a bus named the Prairie Schooner; Joanie and Frank, two con artists; and Hobo Joe. During the journey they are hunted by the police and pursued by the Undertaker. Chivalry, Montana, turns out to be a mining ghost town, and the mystery concerning Worm's real father is revealed. Max realizes that "if you stick to the truth you'll be okay, even if the rest of the world thinks you're a liar."

SUGGESTED UNIT ACTIVITIES

This is a thematic unit focusing on courage, trust, self-discovery, and relationships. Two parallel novels of courage, discovery, and triumphs over imperfection provide stories that will engage young readers in examining their own growth, their own questions about self-identity, and how important it is to build strong bonds with people who may at first appear different.

Teachers will discover that this unit provides a context for exploring people and events appropriate for almost any discipline.

Inherent in each discipline are major events, circumstances, and leaders who have influenced the turn of events, developed new knowledge, and raised issues.

1. Introduce the unit through one or more of the following activities:

   - Assign journal writings or class discussions about what courage means (see pages 79-80) and how courage is an integral part of each discipline.

   - Identify significant people who have made contributions to the discipline, those who exhibited courage in their attempts to change thinking or explain the world.

   - Study a biography of one significant individual who helped to shape the discipline.

   - Identify real-world issues or problems directly related to the discipline. Examine how courage provides a foundation for solving these problems.

   - Identify one or more ideas in the discipline that surfaced through the influence of a major event or person.

2. Study a world problem or issue related to one's discipline: Include such activities as

   - What led to the problem? What knowledge is needed to understand and solve the problem?

   - What individual or individuals have had an impact on solving the problem or could have helped to solve the problem? What is or was the role of courage? How do we gain the courage to face reality and work toward solutions?

   - Compose character sketches of individuals, real or imagined, who would have the qualities needed to solve the problem.

3. Make book connections through the following activities:

   - In both novels, the characters have misunderstandings about themselves and their relationships with others. However, through self-discovery and a keen sense of integrity and courage, they come to understand themselves and what relationships mean. Use the two novels to draw parallels between these characters and those significant people being discussed in the unit. Are there similarities? If so, how? What are the differences resulting from age, situation, time and place, and beliefs? Which of these differences have the greatest or the least impact on solving problems?

Additional suggestions for using the books:

- Choose one or two thought-provoking quotes from the story that address integrity or courage. Use in discussions.

- Brainstorm questions to ask the characters about the themes of courage and integrity.

- Prepare character maps of one or more characters that reflect courage or integrity.

- Chart changes in the characters as they face dilemmas of courage.

- Select three incidents in the story and identify what a particular character's (or the reader's) point of view might be.

4. Examine, study, discuss, and write about key concepts such as: leadership, discovery, human nature, truth, diversity, motivation.

5. Connect content and personal development:

These two novels provide a base for studying connections between young adolescents caught up in misunderstandings, poor self-esteem, fear, and mistrust. These human characteristics are like those of significant people who have helped to shape the world, such as Gandhi, Madame Curie, Jonas Salk, Martin Luther King, Jr., Helen Keller, and Benjamin Franklin. Middle grades students do not often connect these individuals with their own questions, concerns, dilemmas, and problems. Character studies would provide an opportunity for middle grades students to learn that the great ideas and skills they now study across disciplines originated within the minds and events of people – past and present.

6. References, biographies, and novels provide extensions for this unit, such as biographies of Martin Luther King, Jr., Ghandi, Einstein, Benjamin Franklin, or Mozart.

7. Parallel units could be developed that focus on a specific event or person, such as

- The cure for smallpox

- Walking on the moon

- The discovery of a number system

- Influential authors such as Mark Twain or Richard Wright.

- Historical figures, such as Anne Frank, John F. Kennedy, or Thomas Jefferson

- A current event such as September 11 or the continuing Middle East Crisis.

Even with his thick, bug-eyed glasses, Paul Fisher can see better than most people. He can see the lies his parents and brother live out day after day. Until the family is forced to move to Tangerine, no one ever listens or pays much attention to Paul. But in Tangerine, even a dorky, practically blind kid can play soccer and become cool.

Paul, who became visually impaired at age five, is surrounded by the lies his parents and brother tell to hide the truth about the past. When the family moves to the strange town of Tangerine, Florida, Paul discovers many truths. The story raises many questions. Why does Paul perceive his brother, Erik, as menacing and dangerous? What is the mystery and truth surrounding Paul's blindness? Just what does Erik have to do with his blindness? Other mysteries, such as the strange occurrences in Paul's subdivision, fill the novel. During the construction of the subdivision, the builders demolished a tangerine grove, but the rains still come each day at 4:00 p.m., just as lightning continues to strike where there once were hills and trees. The story is filled with oddities like never-ending muck fires, swarms of mosquitoes, and a particular house that is struck by lightning again and again.

Moving to Tangerine not only helps Paul discover truths, but he also creates his own identity without the help of his family. His father is completely obsessed with Erik's football career, oblivious to the rest of the world. First, Paul attends Lake Windsor Middle School where his troubles seem to continue. Because of his visual impairment, his mother, has him classified as "handicapped." This classification eventually gets him removed from the one thing he loves – soccer. Luckily for Paul, a strange occurrence causes the portable buildings at his school to fall into a sinkhole. Because of this, he transfers to another school without the handicapped label. It's a school with a rough reputation and an even tougher soccer team. Paul finds his way, not only onto the soccer team, but also with the kids, transforming himself from geek to hero.

The reader, caught up in this strange and unusual tale, will quickly turn the pages to discover how Paul finally "sees" and what act makes Paul a hero. This book will make an impact on adolescents who have lived in the shadows of a perfect sibling. By the end of the story, the reader will be like the soccer fans at Paul's games, cheering long and hard for Paul and his team.

SUGGESTED UNIT ACTIVITIES

This novel, along with *Freak the Mighty* (Unit 12) and *Kelly's Creek* (Unit 14), provides opportunities for a study of individuals who face the challenges of being physically handicapped and the misunderstandings that young people face as they attempt to cope. The stories emphasize that handicaps do not prevent people from being productive citizens.

Teachers or teams could complete a unit using *Tangerine* alone, or it could be used in combination with *Freak the Mighty* and *Kelly's Creek* for a more in-depth study of young people coping with struggles of acceptance.

1. This unit provides a natural context for initial discussions and supplementary readings on physical handicaps, natural stages of puberty, and perhaps the issues that come with those facing these challenges. See pages 79-80 for some of the discussion and journal-writing suggestions that address diversity or differences.

2. Book discussions during the reading:

   - Some might say that *Tangerine* is about appearances – that if things look good from the outside, then everything will be okay. What do you think about that idea? Where do you see it in the book?

- Why does Erik behave as he does?

- Would you like to live in Paul's community? Why or why not? What is strange about it?

- Who would you rather have for a brother, Erik, Mike, or Luis? Why?

- What are your impressions of Paul's mother? How did she change by the end of the book?

- Paul's mother calls Paul legally blind. Think about the idea of seeing past stereotypes and into people's hearts. How was Paul able to do this? What did he see?

- How is Joey's experience at Tangerine Middle School different from Paul's? Why do you think that is?

- Were you surprised when Luis died?

- Would you have kept the paint incident from Paul if you were his parent? How do you think he felt?

- Did Erik get the punishment he deserved? Why or why not?

- Do you feel hopeful for Paul at the end of the book?

- Is Paul a hero? Why or why not?

- *Tangerine* is Edward Bloor's first novel. Would you read another by him? Why or why not?

- Compare the covers of the paperback and the hardcover. Which one do you like better? Which cover is more appealing? Why do you think the publisher made the changes in the cover?

3. Supplementary readings on handicaps may be used to provide an understanding of particular handicaps. As a class, construct a chart that outlines facts and myths.

4. Do a biographical study of a selected individual with a handicap who made major contributions to society, such as Helen Keller, Muhammed Ali, or Mozart.

5. Study the laws that support the handicapped: history of the laws, rights of the individual, career options, and other relevant topics.

6. Study scientific discoveries that have had positive impacts on the handicapped. Produce drawings or descriptions of devices that have helped specific handicaps.

7. Conduct surveys in the school or community that reflect views of the public about the rights of handicapped individuals in the work force, what people do or don't know about specific handicaps, or views about laws that protect the handicapped.

8. Examine other physical features of young people that are perceived by others in the same way handicapped people are perceived, including their misconceptions and fears, such as obesity, different cultures or language, physical features such as height and weight, special interests that are not usually accepted by peers, specific dress fads, and other differences that surface during the young adolescent years. Students may form small groups to identify the misconceptions, discuss how these influence their view of self, and possible strategies for dispelling the myths of being different.

9. Compose one or more of the following:

   • Stories that include one character who is handicapped, including an authentic story of how the character overcomes the misconceptions.

   • News stories that highlight a positive image of a handicapped person.

   • Fact pages about selected handicapped people.

UNIT 14

Kelly's Creek

by
Doris Buchanan
Smith

Crowell-Collier
Press

*Accepting people
who are different is
difficult; however,
learning to accept
and respect
differences is a
critical event in
growing up.*

Nine-year-old Kelly O'Brien lives with his mother, father, and sister. Their house sits on a bluff overlooking a marsh. Behind the house, there is a runlet that connects Kelly's backyard to the creek. The creek is Kelly's favorite place to be. Each day after school, Kelly can hardly wait to get to the creek. He recently met Phillip, a community college student who is doing a study of marine life in the marsh. Phillip has taught Kelly all about the creatures there. Kelly recognizes that when he is in the marsh he feels smart.

The portrait Doris Buchanan Smith paints is of a kid who tries desperately to be successful. However, the conflict in the story is that Kelly's physical, intellectual, emotional, and social abilities are limited because of a learning disability. He has a visual perception problem that he does not understand. The doctor says it is his eyes. Therefore, Kelly wonders why he does not have glasses. He cannot read, write, or ride a bicycle. Kelly sees himself as dumb because he cannot run and think at the same time. When Kelly is hurting inside he forces a grin to cover his feelings and pain.

Kelly is in a special education class part of the day. When he is in class he has a problem sitting still. Being still sometimes takes all his energy. On one particular day he had to force himself to be still. When his arm kept moving across his desktop, he said to his arm, "Be still. You will get me in trouble." Kelly was already in plenty of trouble. His last progress report had shown no progress. His parents restricted him from visiting the creek. After this, his teacher sent daily reports to his parents. Kelly's learning exercises include templates of a circle, triangle, and square, which he traces with his finger. These experiences help his brain and hands learn to work together.

Phillip is Kelly's only real friend. Phillip convinces Kelly's mother that Kelly should tell his class about the marsh. Kelly does, and he is brilliant. He knows more about the marsh than anyone in his classroom. After this, Kelly's daily reports show improvement. Slowly, Kelly gains the confidence in himself he needs.

SUGGESTED UNIT ACTIVITIES

Teachers may find this book especially useful as a way to construct a novel study in language arts or reading. The book is so powerful that this unit focuses on the story itself, with supplementary enrichment activities that could be developed in social studies, science, career explorations, or health.

1. This unit could begin with a survey or class discussion that focuses on what young adolescents believe to be central issues regarding their interactions with peers, with specific emphasis on self-worth, peer relationships, and other dilemmas they experience as young adolescents.

2. This book is so rich in sound we recommend it be read aloud to students with discussions at strategic places. Following are some questions that seem appropriate for discussion as the book is being read:

   • What does it mean to be different? What is good or difficult about being different?

   • What is it about you – or Kelly – that is misunderstood? How can that happen?

   • Why was Kelly perceived as a misfit? Why did some treat him as different and to some degree incapable of success?

   • Describe a time when being different led to problems in your life.

   • Which of Kelly's traits do you admire? Why?

   • Identify Kelly's actions that are not so different from those you have taken at one time or another? What did you do? How did you feel?

3. Identify specific aspects of the book – or the topic of being different – that small groups or individuals can explore, such as

- Designing school activities that you could do to assist those with handicaps or special needs.

- Interviewing someone who is comfortable with discussing how he or she is different – language, culture, or handicap. What did this person do or say that made him or her feel comfortable being different.

- Researching a person or place that is culturally different. What is it about the place or person that you admire? Why?

- Identifying a personal talent or area of specialized knowledge that makes you different from most of your peers. Describe that talent or demonstrate that expertise.

- Designing TV ads, creating TV characters, writing a story, script, or other creative product that presents a realistic view of someone who is handicapped.

4. Composing a sequel in the form of a short story to *Kelly's Creek* that captures Kelly in a different light – a young man who continues to have a learning disability, yet who is self-confident, accepted by his peers, and has learned to adapt to his handicap.

5. Composing a sequel that tells of Kelly as a confident adult.

6. Designing additional units of study that capture the meaning of the novel, such as

- A study of story writing, focused on the message in the novel.

- Searching for other young adolescent novels, biographies, or other readings that could be read to extend the story of a handicapped individual. Provide a plan for enrichment activities using the additional books.

- In health or science classes developing a thorough unit of study that focuses on handicaps. Include a study of the problem, laws associated with the handicap, and careers for the handicapped.

- In social studies develop a thorough unit on famous people in history, such as Franklin Roosevelt, who have overcome handicaps to make their contributions.
- Develop a study of other countries and how they differ in their perceptions of handicapped individuals, laws, and careers.
- Develop a comprehensive plan for your school or community that recognizes the positive roles that people with handicaps could serve. Develop strategies that focus on making changes to accommodate those with handicaps.

A. Questions for journal writing or class discussion

1. What is special about you? What makes these features special?

2. What opportunities do you have to be yourself? What would you like to be able to do that you have not had the chance to do?

3. What one personal quality do you feel you have that you especially like? Why?

4. What is one thing about you that you would like to change? How can you make the change?

5. What have you accomplished that caused others to be proud of you? Why?

6. Have you ever been asked to do something that you were not sure you could do? What did you do?

7. How can making mistakes help you? Describe a time when this was true.

8. What do you feel you can do that very few people know about?

9. Have you ever been in a position where you were pressured to do something that you knew was wrong? How did you deal with this?

10. What are some things you do or actions you take consistently that show your strength and courage?

11. Is pleasing your friends or pleasing yourself more difficult? Why?

12. Do you see adults behaving in ways that confuse you about what is right and what is wrong? Identify a few.

13. What do you feel are some workable strategies to employ when you are presented with a choice that may not be acceptable by others?

14. Is it ever difficult to be fair? What does being fair mean? What are some dilemmas or conflicts that you felt were unfair? How did they affect you? Who should decide what is fair and what is unfair? Why?

15. Describe an event when you reacted in a way that you wished you had not. How do you wish you had reacted?

16. What have you done recently that caused you to think differently or that changed you or your beliefs?

17. Have you ever learned anything from a friend or family member that you feel was just as important as something you learned in school? What did you learn? From whom?

18. Do individuals your age feel comfortable asking adults personal questions? Why? What adults treat you seriously?

19. How difficult is it to express what you believe? With whom do you feel comfortable in expressing yourself? Why?

20. When you accomplish a difficult task, how do you feel? Why? When you struggle with a task, how do you feel? Is it acceptable to feel frustrated when you struggle with a task? Why?

21. Can you be courageous without being honest? Explain.

B. Enrichment activities and projects

1. Compose a "brag page" celebrating your special accomplishments or the accomplishments of someone else.

2. Demonstrate a talent or skill that you possess but have not demonstrated in school before.

3. Identify a goal you would like to accomplish. Keep a log of the progress toward accomplishing this goal.

4. Select one of your heroes. What qualities make the person heroic? Who are some of your heroes? Why?

5. Prepare a speech for class or write a letter to a local newspaper expressing how and why young people can become involved in community projects.

6. You have been placed in charge of a community project. Plan it and outline your responsibilities. How will you determine if the project is a success?

7. Select a task that is difficult for you. Try it. Explain how you sustained the motivation to accomplish the task.

8. Look through the newspaper to identify situations where people make decisions. Judge whether or not the "right" decision was made. Explain why.

9. Design a code of ethics for a winner and a loser.

10. Interview other students or people from the community. Determine what they view as the most difficult decisions they had to make. What did you find?

11. Design a slogan or short message to encourage others your age to be more responsible for their actions.

12. Compose a story that reflects teenage characters involved in making a decision about right and wrong. Construct two endings – one where the decision was a good one and one where the decision was an unacceptable one.

13. Write a fable about fairness. Create characters who express their emotions.

14. Make a picture collage that illustrates courage.

15. Design a newspaper page that includes cartoons, feature articles, and editorials that address what it takes to be proud of oneself.

16. Compose five questions that would be interesting to explore about what you consider to be a courageous act.

17. Design a poster that reflects a myth about courage.

18. Select a mystery of the world or a problem. Why is it a mystery or problem? What would be two ways to solve the mystery or problem in an honorable way?

19. Identify a career. What does it take for a person in that career to do a job well and maintain integrity?

20. Describe some historical events that illustrated a lack of integrity.

21. Scientists have continued to work to discover answers to questions about health, environment, and diseases. What is one question you would like to discover an answer to and why?

22. Assume you are responsible for helping others. What can you do to help them become responsible individuals? Prepare a guide for them.

23. Construct a timeline over a month that records any actions you take to show integrity or courage. Which one do you feel had the most significance? Why?

C. Responses applicable to all books

1. Give students a synopsis of the storyline. Have students project how they might feel or react in a situation similar to that of a character in the story.

2. Have students connect an episode in their lives to that of the character(s) in the selection.

3. Point out historical events or geographical features in the selection. This may assist in relating the story to other areas of the curriculum.

4. Have students express their views about an issue in the selection. How do they feel about the issue?

5. Make three columns on chart paper. The columns should reflect "Know," "Want to Know," and "Learned." Use the process to link the book to central concepts in the selected discipline.

6. Create a story pyramid to reflect the central problem in the story (problem linked to a problem in a discipline, main events in the story that shows the problem unfolding, and the resolution to the problem).

7. Develop a character yearbook that sketches each character, how the character faces a problem, and how the problem is connected to an authentic situation in his or her life.

8. Organize literature circles to read and respond to the book during the unit (see Harvey Daniels, www.literaturecircles.com). This process provides opportunities for students to read and respond in small groups to multiple books being read, with each group reading a different, but related book, and opportunities for the teacher to read a new book along with students.

9. Keep a log of content learned in a selected discipline from book selections and activities within each unit.

10. Conduct book talks centered around a selected advisory theme such as trust, or a content theme such as the Depression.

D. Additional young adolescent literature for the "Courage and Integrity Theme"

- *Roll of Thunder, Hear My Cry,* by Mildred Taylor

- *One-Eyed Cat,* by Paula Fox

- *Blubber,* by Judy Blume

- *Killing Mr. Griffin,* by Lois Duncan

- *Philip Hall Likes Me, I Reckon Maybe,* by Bette Greene

- *A Taste of Blackberries,* by Doris Buchanan Smith

- *How Many Miles to Babylon?* by Paul Fox

- *The Diary of Anne Frank,* by Frances Goodrich and Albert Hackett

- *Zia,* by Scott O'Dell

- *Julie of the Wolves,* by Jean Craighead George

- *Sweetly Sings the Donkey*, by Vera Cleaver

4. A Guide for Constructing Teacher-Based Advisory Units Across the Curriculum

In order to blend advisory and instruction in various disciplines, connections between the concerns of young adolescents and the major concepts and skills in the academic curriculum have to be identified. As discussed in Chapter 1, these units may become a part of one or more disciplines or may be a central part of the language arts or reading curriculum, with content extensions in science, social studies, mathematics, and exploratory areas. The following guide provides a process for identifying those connections and constructing appropriate units.

Step 1: Identify content concepts, themes, and skills that provide a context for advisory themes.

Examples: A study of any country provides a natural context for considering ways that place affects our customs, relationships, viewpoints , and values and assists young adolescents in understanding diversity, relationships with those who are different, or examination of one's values. There are also many novels that include characters from other ethnic and cultural backgrounds and take place in other countries.

Concepts/Themes/Skills:_____

_____

Step 2: Identify advisory themes that connect to significant content concepts and essential skills.

Examples: Self-identity, establishing relationships with peers, respecting differences, adapting to change, conflict resolution.

Advisory theme(s):_____

Step 3: Identify a context for the unit.

Examples: Many units may be carried out within a single discipline such as a social studies unit on the Depression, language arts/reading unit on a novel, or a study of story elements; or in a multidisciplinary unit in social studies and science focusing on stories set in an arid region of the world that provides significant information about weather, survival, or diverse customs; or in a unit that centers on a young adolescent theme, such as loyalty, which has connections to many disciplines as we study famous historical figures, writers, and scientists.

Discipline(s):_____

Step 4: Identify a young adolescent novel that addresses key content concepts and advisory themes.

Example: *Children of the River* by Linda Crew is a natural for a geography unit to teach how location influences customs, beliefs, and careers. It is a great book to emphasize the importance of understanding diversity and how to relate to those from diverse backgrounds.

Name of novel:_____

Step 5: Plan unit activities from these possibilities:

I. Introductory journal writings or class discussions to establish a framework for integrating advisory themes and content concepts. Entries could be questions that begin to connect content themes or concepts to the personal development of young adolescents, such as questions that help young adolescents begin to think about young men going off to war during World War II.

Example: Have you ever experienced a time when you feared a new place, such as school, community, country? What did you fear? How did you deal with that fear? If you were about to go to war, what would be some of your fears? Have you ever experienced fear when you began a new experience, met new people, or faced something unfamiliar to you?

Activities:_____

II. Keep a journal as you read, listing questions that would connect the book to the content concepts and advisory themes.

The book could be read prior to the unit or in segments as part of the unit. Any young adolescent book should be read by the teacher in advance to determine whether the book would be best read individually by the students, read in small groups, or read aloud to the students. A journal response could be completed in teams of three in response to the following question types: What do you feel you can do to establish stronger relationships with those around you? How do your strategies differ from those actions of the colonists? from cultural group settings in our cities? From the characters in *Seedfolks* who experience cultural differences?

Journal writings/Discussion questions:_____
_____

III. Develop unit activities that focus on each of the following purposes:

- To engage students in the plot, characters, and themes in the young adolescent novel. Example: How did Kelly in *Kelly's Creek* attempt to gain self-confidence?

- To engage students in connecting the content concepts to the plot, characters, and themes in the novel. Example: What motivated Martin Luther King, Jr. to give his speech "I Have a Dream" at a time when the U.S. was unwilling to accept minorities into the mainstream of life in America?

- To engage students in connecting the young adolescent book with content concepts and advisory themes. Example: Compare the actions of King to a character or to one time you made a comment that you knew might not be the most popular point to make with your friends or family. What motivated you?

Such activities serve as the nucleus of a unit and provide a context for merging the major concepts and skills within a selected discipline(s) to a parallel advisory theme. For instance, if you are teaching the features of a particular area in a geography class, such as physical features, one could engage students in discussing how the features affect the livelihood of those who live there and draw parallels to how young people have to adapt to their own surroundings or how the characters in a book adapted to their surroundings. This provides an excellent way to link characters in young adolescent books to the reader. The intent is to identify important ideas from each discipline and determine their connections to parallel experiences in the lives of young adolescents.

The themes, characters, conflicts, and settings in books are reflections of many of the concepts we teach in the various disciplines. What is often overlooked is that what is perceived as important information has a more profound meaning when it is connected to the question, "Why do we teach those facts?"

Activities for 1, 2, and 3:_____

_____

IV. Identify activities that focus specifically on content concepts and activities that merge with advisory themes and connect to the intellectual, social, emotional, and moral development of young people. It is important to identify a sequence in order to provide a natural connection, rather than use the advisory activities as a means to introduce or culminate the unit. Optimum effect is achieved when these are blended into the unit as it progresses.

Content/skill activities:_____

V. Develop activities that engage students in their own learning.

- Responses in the journals or class discussions

- Activities that lead to reflection, inquiry, or problem solving

- Activities that emphasize connections to real life issues or problems

- Activities that involve some individual, small group, and partnership learning

Activities for student involvement:_____

_____

VI. Provide opportunities for students to form stronger connections as the unit ends. Culminating activities should be those that connect what is learned within the discipline to the advisory themes reflected in the unit activities and the young adolescent novel.

- Culminating questions for discussion or journal writing
- Individual or class projects
- Unit extensions: connecting to other concepts or books.

Culminating activities/Projects/Extensions:_____

_____

Conclusion

Central to connecting content to advisory themes and young adolescent novels is the recognition that within each discipline there are concepts and skills that transcend the discipline, ideas that connect to people and events basic to personal development, and ideas that connect some of the issues and concerns expressed by young adolescents to our past, present, and future.

As teachers, regardless of our discipline, we seek to provide instruction that gives purpose to what we teach. Purpose to many young people resides in the questions and concerns that occupy their thoughts. If we are sensitive to how concepts in our content relate to the lives of young people, then integrating content with advisory becomes a natural part of the instructional program in any middle school. ⌐

References

Beane, J.A. (1997). *Curriculum integration: Designing the core of democratic education.* New York: Teachers College Press.

Carnegie Council on Adolescent Development. (1989). *Turning points: Preparing American youth for the 21st century.* New York: Carnegie Corporation.

Jackson, A.W., and Davis, G.A. (2000). *Turning points 2000: Educating adolescents in the 21st century.* New York: Teachers College Press.

James, M., & Spradling, N. (2001). *From advisory to advocacy: Meeting every student's needs.* Westerville, OH: National Middle School Association.

National Council for the Social Studies (1997). Teacher standards: National standards for social studies teachers. Retrieved January 8, 2004, from http://www.socialstudies.org/standards/teachers

National Middle School Association. (2003). *This we believe: Successful schools for young adolescents.* Westerville, OH: Author.

National Research Council. (1996). *National science education standards.* Washington, DC: National Academies Press.

Sheppard, R., & Stratton, B. (1993). *Reflections on becoming: Fifteen literature-based units for the young adolescent.* Columbus, OH: National Middle School Association.

Bibliography of Selected Books for Young Adolescents

Avi. (1992). *The true confessions of Charlotte Doyle.* New York: Avon Books.

Babbitt, N. (1975). *Tuck everlasting.* New York: Farrar, Straus, Giroux.

Bauer, M. (1977). *Foster child.* Minneapolis, MN: The Seabury Press, Inc.

Benjamin, C. (1982). *The wicked stepdog.* New York: Crowell-Collier.

Bloor, E. (2001). *Tangerine.* New York: Scholastic Signature.

Bloss, J. (1990). *A gathering of days.* New York: Aladdin.

Blume, J. (1970). *Are You there God? It's me, Margaret.* New York: E.P. Dutton.

Blume, J. (1971). *Deenie.* New York: Bradbury Press.

Blume, J. (1971). *Then again, maybe I won't.* New York: Bradbury Press.

Blume, J. (1972). *Tales of a fourth grade nothing.* New York: E. P. Dutton.

Blume, J. (1974). *Blubber.* New York: Bradbury Press.

Blume, J. (1981). *The one in the middle is the green kangaroo.* New York: Bradbury Press.

Blume, J. (1981) *Tiger eyes.* New York: Bradbury Press.

Bridgers, S.E. (1957). *Home before dark.* New York: Random House.

Brink, C. (1973). *Caddie Woodlawn.* New York: Macmillan.

Burch, R. (1966). *Queenie Peavy.* New York: Viking Penguin.

Byars, B. (1970). *Summer of the swans.* New York: Viking Penguin.

Byars, B. (1974). *After the goat man.* New York: Viking Penguin.

Byars, B. (1980). *The night swimmers.* New York: Delacorte Press.

Byars, B. (1981). *The Cybil war.* New York: Viking Penguin, Inc.

Byars, B. (1982). *The animal, vegetable, and John D. Jones.* New York: Delacorte Press.

Byars, B. (1985). *Cracker Jackson.* New York: Viking Penguin.

Clapp, P. (1977). *I'm Deborah Sampson: A soldier in the war of the revolution.* New York: Lothrop, Lee and Shepard.

Cleary, B. (1968). *Ramona the pest.* New York: William Morrow and Company.

Cleary, B. (1973). *Me too.* Philadelphia: J. B. Lippincott.

Cleary, B. (1977). *Ramona and her father.* New York: William Morrow and Company.

Cleary, B. (1983). *Dear Mr. Henshaw.* New York: William Morrow and Company.

Cleaver, V. (1985). *Sweetly sings the donkey.* New York: Harper and Row.

Cleaver, V., & Cleaver, B. (1969). *Where the lilies bloom.* Philadephia: J. B. Lippincott.

Cleaver, V., & Cleaver, B. (1978). *Queen of hearts.* Philadelphia, PA: J.B. Lippincott.

Crane, S. (1962). *The red badge of courage.* New York: Norton.

Creech, S. (1996). *Walk two moons.* New York: HarperCollins.

Creech, S. (2002). *The wanderer.* New York: HarperCollins.

Crew, L. (1991). *Children of the river.* New York: Laurel Leaf Library.

Cunningham, J. (1970). *Burnish me bright.* New York: Pantheon Books,.

Curtis, C.P. (1995). *The Watsons go to Birmingham.* New York: Bantam Doubleday Dell.

Curtis, C.P. (2002). *Bud, not buddy.* New York: Random House Books.

Danzinger, P. (1978). *The pistachio prescription.* New York: Delacorte Press.

Danzinger, P. (1979). *Can you sue your parents for malpractice?* New York: Delacorte Press.

DeClements, B. (1981). *Nothing's fair in fifth grade.* New York: Viking Press.

dePaola, T. (1973). *Nana upstairs, Nana downstairs.* New York: G.P. Putnam Sons.

dePaola, T. (1983). *The legend of the bluebonnet.* New York: G. P. Putnam Sons.

Dowell, F. O. (2001). *Dovey Coe.* New York: Aladdin Paperbacks.

Duncan, L. (1978). *Killing Mr. Griffin.* Boston: Little, Brown and Company.

Fleischman, P. (1998). *Seedfolks.* New York: HarperCollins Children's Books.

Flourney, V. (1985). *The patchwork quilt.* New York: Dial Books for Young Readers.

Fox, P. (1984). *One-eyed cat.* New York: Bradbury Press.

Fox, P. (1967). *How many miles to Babylon?* Chicago: Independent Publishers Group.

Fritz, J. (1987). *The cabin faced west.* New York: Puffin Books.

George, J.C. (1959). *My side of the mountain.* New York: E. P. Dutton.

George, J.C. (1972). *Julie of the wolves.* New York: Harper and Row.

George, J.C. (1983). *The talking earth.* New York: Harper and Row.

Goble, P. (1978). *The girl who loved wild horses.* New York: Bradbury Press.

Goodrich, F., & Hackett, A. (1956). *The diary of Anne Frank.* New York: Houghton Mifflin.

Greene, B. (1973). *Summer of my German soldier.* New York: Dial Press.

Greene, B. (1974). *Philip Hall likes me. I reckon maybe.* New York: Dial Press.

Greene, B. (1976). *Beat the turtle drum.* New York: Viking Press.

Greene, C. (1972). *The unmaking of Rabbit.* New York: Viking Penguin.

Greene, C. (1974). *The ears of Louis.* New York: Viking Penguin.

Greene, C. (1977). *Getting nowhere.* New York: Viking Penguin, Inc.

Haley, A. (1976). *Roots.* New York: Doubleday.

Hamilton, V. (1967). *Zeely.* New York: Macmillan

Hamilton, V. (1971). *The planet of Junior Brown.* New York: Macmillan.

Hobbs, W. (1995). *Downriver.* New York: Laurel Leaf Library.

Holt, K.W. (2001). *When Zachary Beaver came to town.* New York: Yearling.

Klein, N. (1972). *Mom, the wolfman and me.* New York: Pantheon Books.

Konigsburg, E. L. (1967). *From the mixed up files of Mrs. Basil E. Frankweiler.* NewYork: Anthenum.

Little, J. (1968). *Take wing.* Boston: Little, Brown and Company.

Lowry, L. (1979). *Anastasia Krupnik.* Boston: Houghton Mifflin.

Lowry, L. (1982). *Thirteen ways to sink a sub.* New York: Lothrop, Lee, and Shepard.

Lowry, L.. (1994). *The giver.* New York: Laurel Leaf Library.

MacLachlan, P. (1985). *Sarah, plain and tall.* New York: Harper and Row.

Mann, P. (1973). *My Dad lives in a downtown hotel.* New York: Doubleday and Company.

Mann, P. (1977). *There are two kinds of terrible.* New York: Doubleday and Company.

Myers, W.D. (1978). *It ain't all for nothing.* New York: Viking Penguin.

Myers, W.D. (2001). *Monster.* New York: HarperCollins Children's Books.

O'Dell S. (1960). *Island of the blue dolphins.* Boston, MA: Houghton Mifflin.

O'Dell S. (1976). *Zia.* Boston: Houghton Mifflin.

Paterson, K. (1977). *Bridge to Terabithia.* New York: Crowell-Collier Press.

Paterson, K. (1980). *Jacob have I loved.* New York: Crowell-Collier Press.

Paterson, K. (1985). *Come sing, Jimmy Jo.* New York: Crowell-Collier Press.

Paterson, K. (1992). *Lyddie.* New York: Puffin Books.

Paterson, K. (1984). *Tracker.* New York: Scholastic.

Paulson, G. (1985). *Dogsong.* New York: Bradbury Press.

Paulson, G. (1987). *Hatchet.* New York: Bradbury Press.

Paulson, G. (1990). *Woodsong.* New York: Bradbury Press.

Peck, R. (1985). *Remembering the good times.* New York: Delacorte Press.

Peck, R. (2000). *A year down yonder.* New York: Penguin Putnam Books.

Pfeiffer, S.B. (1981). *What do you do when your mouth won't open?* New York: Delacorte Press.

Philbrick, R. (1993). *Freak the mighty.* New York: Scholastic Systems.

Philbrick, R. (1998). *Max the mighty.* New York: Point Signature.

Rawls, W. (1987). *Where the red fern grows.* Santa Barbara, CA: ABC-CLIO.

Reeder, C. (1999). *Shades of gray.* New York: Aladdin Paperbacks.

Sachar, L. (2000). *Holes.* New York: Yearling.

Seabrooke, B. (1980). *Home is where they take you in.* New York: William Morrow and Company.

Smith, D.B. (1973). *A taste of blackberries.* New York: Crowell-Collier Press.

Smith, D.B. (1975). *Kelly's creek.* New York: Crowell-Collier Press.

Smith, R.K. (1984). *The war with Grandpa.* New York: Delacorte Press.

Speare, E. (1983). *Sign of the beaver.* Boston, MA: Houghton Mifflin.

Sperry, A. (1969). *Sounder.* New York: Harper and Row.

Spinelli, J. (1990). *Maniac Magee.* Boston: Little, Brown and Company.

Staples, S.F. (1991). *Shabanu: Daughter of the wind.* New York: Alfred A. Knopf.

Staples, S.F. (1993). *Haveli.* New York: Knopf

Taylor, M. (1976). *Roll of thunder, hear my cry.* New York: Dial Pess.

Voight, C. (1982). *Dicey's song.* New York: Atheneum Publishers.

Yep, L. (1975). *Dragonwings.* New York: Scholastic.

Literature Web Sites

http://www.ala.org/srrt/csking/index.html

www.nationalbook.org)

www.ipl.org/ref/litcrit/

www.childrenstory.com/tales/index.htm)

http://www.edupaperback.org/top100.html

http://www.geocities.com/EnchantedForest/5165/index1.html

http://www.carr.lib.md.us/mae/myer/myers.htm

www.st-charles.lib.il.us/low/ythread.htm

www.writerlady.com

http://falcon.jmu.edu/~ramseyil/sachar.htm

http://scils.rutgers.edu/~kvander/myers.html

http://dcls.org/x/archives/poe.html

www.carolhurst.com

http://www.englishcompanion.com/

http://www.k-1.com/Orwell/

http://www.afn.org/~afn15301/drseuss.html

www.bham.wednet.edu/bio/biomaker.htm

About the Authors

Ronnie Sheppard, chair of the Department of Teaching and Learning at Georgia Southern University, is co-author of the 1993 NMSA publication *Reflections on Becoming: Fifteen Literature-Based Units for the Young Adolescent,* and an earlier monograph. Dr. Sheppard, a former member of NMSA's Publications Committee, has been a presenter each year since 1976 at NMSA's annual conference and has conducted over one hundred workshops on teaching language arts, writing, reading, integrated curriculum, and interdisciplinary teaming in middle schools in Georgia and Texas. He is also the editor for Georgia Middle School Association's monograph series.

Kim Ruebel, assistant professor of Middle Grades Education at Georgia Southern University, has written numerous articles for *Middle School Journal.* A former teacher at the elementary and middle grades levels in Indiana, Dr. Ruebel teaches methods courses in young adolescent literature, writing instruction, and middle school methods; she works extensively with middle schools in Georgia as a language arts, reading, and writing consultant.

Katie Sheppard is a sixth-grade team leader and language arts teacher at Langston Chapel Middle School in Statesboro, Georgia. She taught language arts and social studies to young adolescents in grades 5-8 for over 30 years. She has made numerous presentations at National Middle School Association conferences and has served as a consultant to middle schools in Texas and Georgia.

Beverly Stratton recently retired as chair of the Department of Early Childhood and Reading at Georgia Southern University. Dr. Stratton, co-author of the 1993 publication of *Reflections on Becoming: Fifteen Literature-Based Units for the Young Adolescents* was a reading specialist for grades five and six for many years in Ohio before joining the faculty at Georgia Southern in 1983.

Diane Zigo, assistant professor of English Education at Buffalo SUNY, formerly taught at Georgia Southern University where she served as a literature and writing consultant for middle grades in Georgia. Dr. Zigo has published numerous articles in leading language arts journals and has also served in leadership roles for the National Council for Teachers of English. Her specialty is in teaching language arts and reading to diverse learners.

National Middle School Association

National Middle School Association, established in 1973, is the voice for professionals and others interested in the education and well-being of young adolescents. The association has grown rapidly and enrolls members in all 50 states, the Canadian provinces, and 42 other nations. In addition, 57 state, regional, and provincial middle school associations are official affiliates of NMSA.

NMSA is the only national association dedicated exclusively to the education, development, and growth of young adolescents. Membership is open to all. While middle level teachers and administrators make up the bulk of the membership, central office personnel, college and university faculty, state department officials, other professionals, parents, and lay citizens are members and active in supporting our single mission – improving the educational experiences of 10-15 year olds. This open and diverse membership is a particular strength of NMSA s.

The association publishes *Middle School Journal,* the movement s premier professional journal; *Research in Middle Level Education Online; Middle Ground, the Magazine of Middle Level Education; The Family Connection,* an online newsletter for families; *Classroom Connections,* a practical quarterly resource; and a series of research summaries.

A leading publisher of professional books and monographs in the field of middle level education, NMSA provides resources both for understanding and advancing various aspects of the middle school concept and for assisting classroom teachers in planning for instruction. More than 120 professional publications dealing with all phases of middle level education are included in the resource catalog and can be ordered online.

The association s highly acclaimed annual conference has drawn many thousands of registrants every fall. NMSA also sponsors numerous other professional development opportunities.

For information about NMSA and its many services, contact the association s headquarters office at 4151 Executive Parkway, Suite 300, Westerville, Ohio, 43081. TELEPHONE: 800-528-NMSA; FAX: 614-895-4750; INTERNET: www. nmsa.org.